SMUGGLERS, BOOTLEGGERS, AND SCOFFLAWS

SMUGGLERS, BOOTLEGGERS, AND SCOFFLAWS

Prohibition and New York City

Ellen NicKenzie Lawson

excelsior editions
State University of New York Press
Albany, New York

Excelsior Editions is an imprint of State University of New York Press

For information, contact State University of New York Press, Albany, NY
www.sunypress.edu

Production by Cathleen Collins
Marketing by Kate McDonnell

Library of Congress Cataloging-in-Publication Data

Lawson, Ellen NicKenzie.
  Smugglers, bootleggers, and scofflaws : prohibition and New York City / Ellen
NicKenzie Lawson.
    pages cm
  Includes bibliographical references and index.
  ISBN 978-1-4384-4816-9 (paperback : alkaline paper)
  1. Prohibition—New York (State)—New York—History—20th century.
2. Crime—New York (State)—New York—History—20th century.   3. Criminals—
New York (State)—New York—History—20th century.   4. Smugglers—New York
(State)—New York—History—20th century.   5. New York (N.Y.)—Social
conditions—20th century.   I. Title.

  HV5090.N7L39 2013
  363.4'109747109042—dc23   2012044468

10 9 8 7 6 5 4 3 2 1

In honor of Mary and Paul Mangelsdorf

CONTENTS

ILLUSTRATIONS

AUTHOR'S NOTE

"New York City, as the greatest liquor market in the United States, is a great temptation for the rum runners," a Coast Guard Intelligence officer wrote in the eighth year of Prohibition.[1]

Smugglers to New York City succeeded in bringing liquor ashore despite the vigilance of the Coast Guard, Customs, and local authorities, including the harbor police. Liquor syndicates, initially organized in ethnic neighborhoods in lower Manhattan, distributed smuggled liquor throughout the city. These same syndicates also controlled illegal breweries, diverted liquor dedicated to industrial and medicinal use from licensed distilleries, and organized home-made wine and gin operations.

Smuggled and bootlegged liquor supplied the city's 500 night clubs and 30,000 speakeasies. A new word, coined in a national contest in the fifth year of Prohibition, described those frequenting these clubs and speakeasies as "scofflaws." There were hundreds of thousands of scofflaws in the nation's largest city.[2]

A unique, extensive, little-used database of information on liquor smuggling to New York City exists in the National Archives among Coast Guard records. This book utilizes significant, new information and photographs from this valuable, historic source.[3]

Linking together smuggling, bootlegging, and scofflaw history for New York City is essential to understand the failure of the 18th Amendment. Resistance to Prohibition is not usually a serious subject in U.S. history. Many scholars are merely amused that Prohibition ever existed, embarrassed that the Amendment was ratified, appalled that it gave a boost to organized crime, and relieved that it was repealed.

Nevertheless, Repeal was a significant event in U.S. history—one of the few times that "We the people" acknowledged having erred. In this it is on a par with two other major historical events—the creation of the Constitution in 1787 and the ratification of the 13th Amendment at the end of the Civil War. In the first case, the nation recognized that the government formed under the Articles of Confederation was a failure. In the second case, the nation recognized that the original Constitution was a pro-slavery document and needed to be amended. And finally in 1933, for the very first and only time, the nation repealed a constitutional amendment.

The history of Al Capone in Chicago during Prohibition has long fascinated the American public, but New York City remained the nation's largest liquor market. Drys, meaning those who supported Prohibition, considered New York City as "Babylon-on-the-Hudson," given the many languages spoken by its immigrants, and "Satan's Seat," given its corrupt Democratic political machine (Tammany Hall) and its decadent Bowery and Tenderloin districts. Drying up New York City promised to be the Drys' greatest triumph, but instead the city remained determinedly Wet.[4]

This book brings together three strands of Prohibition history. First, there is the untold story of liquor smuggling to New York City, based on information on 250 rumrunning vessels seized by the U.S. Coast Guard along with many unpublished agency photographs. Second, although individual histories of Italian-American, Jewish-American, and Irish-American gangs for New York City exist, until now there has been no coherent narrative of the rise of large-scale organized crime out of the liquor syndicates in these neighborhoods. Third, information on 150 of Manhattan's best-known speakeasies and night clubs shows an incredible diversity attracting residents, tourists, and visiting businesspeople to explore the entire city.

Congressman Fiorello La Guardia, Mayor James J. Walker, Governor Al Smith, Columbia University President Nicholas Murray Butler, Republican National Committeewoman Pauline Morton Sabin, philanthropist John D. Rockefeller Jr., and finally Democratic Presidential "New Deal" candidate Franklin Delano Roosevelt, all of them New Yorkers, provided the national leadership ending Prohibition.

I could not have researched this subject without the invaluable assistance of interlibrary loan librarians in public libraries in Colorado. I am especially appreciative of the staff at the National Archives in Washington D.C. for assistance with the Coast Guard Seized Vessel

Records, 1920–1933. In addition, I especially valued the published histories of Malcolm Willoughby, Carl Sifakis, and Michael Lerner.

Field Horne, program chair for the 2008 New York State History Conference in Saratoga Springs, recognized the importance of rumrunning and New York City by including my initial paper on this topic in that conference. I also wish to thank Jim Worsham, editor of publications for the National Archives, Mary Ryan, managing editor of *Prologue: Journal of the National Archives*, and writer Benjamin Guterman for publishing a summary of this manuscript, with extensive illustrations, in the fall 2011 issue of *Prologue*.

Dave Talbott's advice, in the initial stages of writing, Deborah Hoffman's invaluable editing experience and friendship, Mary and Steve Cremins' suggestion of a helpful source on Irish-American bootleggers, and former student Devery Anderson's editing assistance, were deeply appreciated. I am thankful to Dr. Alea Henle, my daughter, for suggesting New York City as the focus for research, and to son Josh Medley for his support. Finally, editors Rafael Chaiken, Amanda Lanne, and Cathleen Collins at SUNY Press, were very helpful in the editing process.

Ellen NicKenzie Lawson, PhD
Colorado, 2013

PREFACE

When the 18th Amendment became law in January 1920, Americans were obliged to abstain from alcohol for purposes of personal enjoyment. Production of alcohol for religious, medicinal, military, or industrial use remained legal. Poisonous or nauseating agents called *denaturants* were added to industrial alcohol to discourage diversion. "Near beer," made by producing real beer and then weakening its alcoholic content, remained legal. The production, transportation, and sale of liquor for personal use was forbidden.[1]

The U.S. Senate spent thirteen hours debating the merits of the Prohibition Amendment before approving it. The House of Representatives considered and approved it in eight hours. The Wartime Prohibition Act, in effect at the end of World War I, enabled many Americans to view Prohibition as merely an extension of a wartime measure. The Progressive Movement, which successfully called for an end to child labor, the regulation of food, meat, and drugs, and the extension of the suffrage to women, was also behind passage of the 18th Amendment as a solution to the perceived abuse of liquor and alcoholism. Industrialists also supported the Dry Amendment to ensure a sober workforce come Monday morning.

On the other hand, those opposed to the amendment were disorganized or effectively silenced. Major German-American brewers were discredited during the war against Germany. Irish immigrants were suspected of less than wholehearted support for the war because Great Britain, an ally, still opposed independence for Ireland. Immigrants from Southern and Eastern Europe, particularly Italians and Jews, brought new political philosophies, such as anarchism and socialism, which were perceived to be un-American. With the war ended and the 18th Amendment ratified, these groups began to assert themselves again.

New York was one of the last states to ratify the amendment, doing so only after enough states had already approved it. The New York State Assembly voted 81 to 66 in favor, and the New York State Senate 27 to 24. Voters outside New York City held disproportionate power in the state legislature because the U.S. Supreme Court did not rule that legislative apportionment must follow a "one man, one vote" principle until the 1960s. Even within the city, Dry forces proved effective lobbyists, convincing some voters it was Progressive to be for a cause that would weaken the Tammany political machine whose organizational strength was in the city's saloons.

In 1920, the population in the United States, unlike New York State, was primarily rural. Many regarded cities as necessary evils, not as harbingers of the future. The 18th Amendment reflected this anti-urban, anti-modern bias. Passed in January 1919, the amendment was not scheduled to take effect until the following January. In October 1919, Congress passed the Volstead Act defining what was covered by the Amendment. Many expected that hard liquor would be banned but not beer and wine. That was not the case.

Prohibition began midnight January 16, 1920. Guests and waiters wore black at New York's Park Avenue Hotel where liquor was served in black glasses. At midnight the ballroom was darkened and a spotlight focused on two couples ceremoniously taking a black bottle from an open coffin in the center of the room, pouring out the last drops, and holding black handkerchiefs to their faces to wipe away tears. At Reisenweber's, a popular Manhattan dance hall, the ballroom orchestra played Chopin's *Funeral March*. One hundred cases of legal champagne were given away at midnight at the Hotel Vanderbilt while an orchestra played "Goodbye Forever."

Wealthy New Yorkers stocked their wine cellars with last-minute purchases and private clubs rented storage space in bonded warehouses. Those who made their living from the production, transportation, and sale of liquor—captains, sailors, longshoremen, owners of saloons and bars, waiters, bartenders, and liquor store owners—wondered how they would make a living in the new era. On the other hand, urban gang leaders and their associates contemplated how to exploit what promised to be a new, highly profitable, black market in liquor.[1]

1

RUM ROW

New York City, the nation's largest liquor market before Prohibition, retained this distinction throughout the Dry era. In the weeks and months prior to January 1920, wealthy city residents stored liquor in bonded warehouses, which they could legally access as long as the supplies lasted. Wholesale liquor dealers shipped liquor not yet sold to the Bahamas to avoid confiscation, slowly smuggling it back. Canadian liquor producers revved up production and eventually supplied the majority of imported liquor to the nation. Soon foreign liquor supply ships from Great Britain, France, Germany, Holland, Italy, Norway, the Bahamas, Cuba, and Canada, stationed off Long Island, New Jersey, Staten Island, and Brooklyn, became known as "Rum Row."[1]

The United States negotiated a treaty with Canada and Great Britain in 1924 to extend the legal limit from three to twelve miles. This made the journey from shore more difficult. Rum Row was now relocated beyond the new limit, southeast of Nantucket and Long Island. A rare nautical chart in the National Archives illustrates Coast Guard documentation of the locations of one supply ship on Rum Row over an entire year. When that ship strayed within the limit, it was seized and this chart was used in court proceedings.[2]

Hundreds of sea captains smuggled liquor to Rum Row but few left records. One who did was Bill McCoy, a New York merchant mariner who began by smuggling liquor from the Bahamas. His biography, published in the final years of Prohibition, sold well because he had the reputation, deserved or not, of smuggling the best liquor, the "real McCoy." He began smuggling in a slow-moving boat that was seized off

1

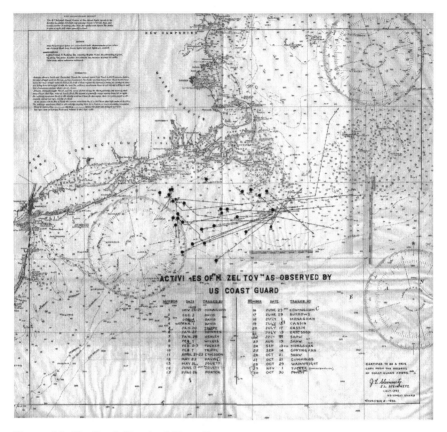

Figure 1.1. Nautical Chart of Rum Row
A Coast Guard chart for 1929–1930 traces the movements of the vessel *Mazel Tov* in the area known as New York's *Rum Row*, more than 12 miles off the New York and New England coasts. Smaller U.S. contact boats smuggled liquor ashore from these international waters. Courtesy of the National Archives.

Atlantic City when he was not aboard, possibly hiding out on Martha's Vineyard among the Wampanoag tribe near Gay Head. At this point he had enough money to buy an expensive, fast-moving, Gloucester-built schooner, which he illegally registered as British to provide immunity from seizure. Despite its British flag, the schooner was known to belong to McCoy and was chased inside the legal limit and boarded. This time he was present and was ordered at gunpoint to proceed to Staten Island. The courts upheld the seizure and his schooner was sold at auction. He managed to get it back, was seized again off the entrance to New York harbor, changed its registration to French, and headed to Bermuda for more liquor. Eventually McCoy served nine months in jail for smuggling. Mabel Walker Willebrandt, Assistant U.S. Attorney General who was responsible for Prohibition enforcement for most of the 1920s, said McCoy's smuggling career proved how difficult it was for authorities to deal with ships under foreign registry. Most supply ships on Rum Row followed McCoy's lead and maintained foreign registration through "dummy" owners because the Coast Guard could not stop or board such ships as long as they stayed beyond the limit.[3]

Nautical Wild West

Rum Row was not well patrolled in its earliest years because the Coast Guard had neither adequate manpower nor a large enough fleet. Until 1925, Rum Row was a nautical version of the American Wild West. Piracies and hijackings were so common that most captains and crews armed themselves. McCoy kept a rifle prominently displayed in his sales room. There were several documented cases of piracy. The earliest was a New York boat whose skipper was bound and gagged at gunpoint and robbed of $23,000 worth of whiskey. Another early piracy involved a New York boat near Martha's Vineyard, in which eight unidentified bodies floated up on the shore, including one with stab wounds. In this case, authorities eventually surmised that pirates rammed the boat in a fog and sank it because they believed they had been double-crossed—and that the pirates owned the cargo of Canadian ale.[4]

More is known about the piracy of a French ship robbed by a New York gang. McCoy had been approached in Manhattan prior to the event by a man named "Eddie" and invited to participate. According to McCoy, Eddie and his associates were angry because a French agent from the ship had arrived in Manhattan to take orders directly and bypassed them. Eddie said, "'American rum-running by Americans,' that's our motto." They decided to wine and dine the agent on Broadway while twenty-four armed pirates motored out from Sheepshead Bay to the ship, shackled its crew in the hold, tied up the officers in the cabins, and forced the captain to move the ship closer to Fire Island. Over the next ten days, they plundered $800,000 worth of liquor using ten smaller boats, many from a marine garage on the East River.[5]

Lloyd's of London had insured the cargo, and as it was a French ship that was pirated, there was an investigation in Paris where French authorities arrested Jerome Max Phaff, a naturalized German-American and former admiralty lawyer who gave his address as 219 East 196th Street, Manhattan. They charged Phaff with complicity even though he had not been on the ship at the time. After seven weeks in a French prison, he told what he knew and was released. A French magistrate told the Associated Press that with Phaff's help they had traced all the liquor exported from France to the United States, and Dry America had had a "very wet spell indeed." Phaff returned to Manhattan after receiving assurance that he might be spared prosecution if he gave information to the U.S. Attorney for the Southern District of New York.[6]

Another documented case of piracy by New Yorkers was a British ship carrying a liquor cargo ordered by the Chelsea Trading Company, located at 42nd Street, Manhattan. The pirates used machine guns, imprisoned the captain, and plundered the ship of $700,000 worth of liquor. Investigations by the London Schooners' Association concluded that the pirates had inside knowledge and that the piracy was an insurance scam.

In one mysterious case, a deserted British ship was sighted floating in the dark off Fire Island. Rifle shells were scattered around the deck. It appeared that the sailors aboard left abruptly as they had not packed any of their clothes. In another case, a ship from Nassau on Rum Row was robbed by forty armed men and ran out of fuel and food after the pirates departed. The skipper decided to gut the interior for wood to fuel the ship, set sail for New York City, and surrendered the ship as a rumrunner. The oddest case of piracy was a boat on Rum Row disguised to look like a Coast Guard patrol boat with the pirates dressed in guardsmen's uniforms. Another fake Coast Guard ship, or perhaps this same one, was later discovered in New York harbor after its crew failed to give the traditional Coast Guard greeting while passing a genuine patrol boat.[7]

Besides pirates, dense fogs could be a danger, especially before radio communications for navigational purposes became common. One captain, lost in a thick fog, feared that he would sail within the legal limit and be caught. To his relief, he discovered his ship surrounded by floating garbage, placing him near the location where New York City regularly dumped its refuse. He knew this place because, when the wind blew from the west, smugglers on Rum Row could smell it.

So he charted his location and sailed back to the Row. At least one New York City garbage scow was eventually seized smuggling liquor on a return trip, and a sewage barge was discovered loaded with liquor off the entrance to New York harbor. On the other hand, fog could also be a friend, allowing rumrunners to evade the Coast Guard.[8]

Storms with strong winds and powerful currents were another danger; these could sink ships or blow them off course. One captain's ship was caught in such a storm that created a funnel with New Jersey on one side and Long Island on the other. While a shipwreck would bring him and crew death, successfully swimming to shore could lead to arrest and jail. Guardsmen also risked their lives at sea while hunting down smugglers. When a rumrunner was seized in a snowstorm off Long Island, the guardsman placed aboard was alone on deck for 36 hours as he steered it back to New York City.[9]

The actual number of rum ships lost at sea during Prohibition, like the number of piracies at sea, will probably never be known. The Coast Guard learned indirectly of a few from grieving families on shore. For example, Agnes McCardle's brother died, along with twelve others, when his rumrunner sank in a storm at sea: the captain was a retired Manhattan policeman. The ship's owner had lost another New York rum boat a few years earlier in a storm. Sixteen men had gone down with that boat. McCardle wanted the owner arrested for using unseaworthy vessels and for refusing to honor the life insurance claims of sailors' families. Four Brooklyn women, including the wives of Gustav Nordstrom and Charles Nordstedt, reported the loss of another ship, also after failed attempts to collect insurance from its owners. In that case, the Coast Guard had already seized a different ship belonging to the same people, and they had been arrested and were soon to be tried.[10]

In the mid-1920s, Rum Row came under the control of well-financed Manhattan gangs with warehouses in the Canadian Maritime provinces and farther north in the French-owned islands of St. Pierre and Miquelon. These gangs used European freighters to bring liquor across the ocean to the warehouses. They also had a fleet of smaller boats bringing the warehoused liquor to Rum Row or transporting liquor directly from Canada, which supplied an estimated 80 percent of smuggled liquor. Fast speedboats, up to thirty-eight miles per hour, were used to deliberately decoy the Coast Guard away while larger ships were transferring the liquor to smaller boats. One of these ships, which was finally seized, belonged to William Duffy who owned Duffy's Tavern on Broadway and managed prize fighters in his spare time. Another was a submarine chaser, built in Buffalo and intended for the Imperial Russian Navy, which became a fast pilot ship for smugglers on Rum Row before returning to the Great Lakes and smuggling across Lake Erie.[11]

Cat and Mouse

A good five years into Prohibition, the U.S. Coast Guard was transformed into a more effective force as a result of a large federal appropriation to modernize the agency, doubling enlisted personnel and adding twenty naval destroyers to its fleet. Eighteen of the destroyers remained on the East Coast, with six stationed at Staten Island near the entrance to New York harbor, six in Connecticut's New London harbor with easy access to Rum Row, and six in Boston. On hearing the news, one leading New York gangster remained unconcerned, reminding subordinates that every man had his price, including guardsmen. He later joked, after he lost a ship in the North Atlantic because it hit an iceberg, that it was too bad he couldn't buy the icebergs.[12]

For the remainder of Prohibition, the Coast Guard and New York smuggling syndicates played cat and mouse on Rum Row. The treaty setting the legal limit never actually specified mileage but was worded "one hour's distance from shore," in a day when most large ships could go no faster than twelve miles per hour. At first, the newly enhanced Coast Guard aggressively interpreted the treaty as referring to U.S. speedboats, which could go up to forty miles an hour. So the Coast Guard seized legitimate foreign ships from England, Holland, Canada, France, and Norway, which hovered less than forty miles out. One Norwegian captain, more than twenty miles out, was ordered to sail to New York harbor where his crew was imprisoned at Ellis Island before being deported. While the case was being litigated, the ship remained in New York harbor. Eventually the Coast Guard lost this case and others like it. Had the courts not upheld the original intent of twelve or so miles, this would have moved Rum Row so far out that it would have been the rare boat from shore that would have made contact.[13]

Another legal decision also strengthened enforcement on Rum Row. This happened after a U.S. judge, hostile to Prohibition, ruled that the Coast Guard had no authority over any ship, including U.S.

ones, beyond the limit. Until the judge was overruled, the Coast
Guard avoided hauling rum ships into his district. Eventually the U.S.
Supreme Court upheld the agency's rights. The Coast Guard, established a few years before Prohibition, replaced the old Revenue Cutter
Service and retained its powers, including stopping the importation
of slaves after 1808, enforcing neutrality laws, and suppressing piracy.
Thus, the Court ruled that the U.S. Coast Guard had the power "to
seize American vessels anywhere on the high seas for violation of any
laws of the United States." Nevertheless, it remained legal for fishing
schooners, which would otherwise be empty outward bound from New
York City, to bring provisions to ships on Rum Row. This enabled
foreign ships to remain on the Row for months instead of having to
return to their own ports for food and water. But it was not legal for
American boats to exchange provisions for liquor and then bring the
liquor to shore. After the Coast Guard seized one such boat, syndicate
lawyers argued the fishing license to trade was inclusive. The courts
ruled such boats could only trade items specified in their license and
liquor was not included.[14]

Given that New York was the greatest liquor market before Prohibition and legally could continue to export liquor abroad during Prohibition, the Coast Guard's focus on New York's Rum Row made sense.
Technically, the agency was responsible for smuggling along five thousand miles of national coastline. Two hundred large vessels were devoted
to detecting smuggling. If the Coast Guard had not concentrated on
the New York market, the agency would have had one Coast Guard
ship for every twenty-five miles of coastline, or given the legal limit,
for three hundred square miles. This was clearly impossible. The most
effective use of the fleet was to patrol Rum Row by day and assign
one destroyer for each large rum ship at night when most smuggling
occurred. Every so often, after a storm or at the dark of the moon, the
agency would conduct a sweep up the entire coast from Virginia to the
Canadian border.[15]

Sometimes Coast Guard monitoring on Rum Row bordered on
harassment of genuine foreign ships. One British captain complained
that his ship had been used for target practice by the U.S. Coast Guard
and a letter went out, "Her Majesty's Government and the Government
of the Dominion of Canada cannot agree that the mere fact of a vessel
being accused by U.S. Authorities of having engaged in the smuggling
trade entitles those authorities to attack or molest her on the high seas."

The Coast Guard backed off but dogged this ship five more years each time it returned to Rum Row. Another time the Coast Guard mistook a British ship in the dark for a U.S. rumrunner, fired at it, and it began to leak. An official apology was soon issued.[16]

Harassment at sea was successful in preventing some ships from discharging any liquor to U.S. contact boats. One Nova Scotia Captain, Charles Lemarois, 48, became despondent about financial reversals over an earlier failed trip and was unwilling to return to his home port after a second one. He committed suicide by jumping overboard in a snowstorm while his crew was at dinner. Another Rum Row life and death drama had a positive ending when a badly burned sailor was transferred to a British liquor ship with a doctor on board. The sailor's condition was stabilized, and he was rushed ashore to Long Island's Rockaway Beach Hospital.[17]

Some foreign ships went over the legal line. Men aboard a British ship tried to bribe guardsmen to bring liquor to shore. After notifying their superiors, guardsmen played along and collected evidence that could be used against the ship in court. Then orders went out to chase the ship over the entire ocean, to the British limit if necessary. The ensuing chase began twenty miles out and lasted twelve hours. Another "foreign" ship, owned by the Staten Island Fox-Levine Gang, was trailed on Rum Row for three years. Its photo, taken from a Coast Guard ship, shows the cat and mouse nature of the "Rum Wars." Eventually, the schooner caught fire and sank off Nantucket, taking a load of champagne to the bottom of the sea.[18]

United States' ships beyond the limit sometimes had legitimate reason for being there, such as carrying coal from Virginia to New England. On occasion, these legitimate vessels were harassed if suspected of picking up liquor as they passed Rum Row. A coal ship, owned by a football coach at Yale, was suspected of picking up liquor at sea. The Coast Guard fired blank shots at it to force it to hove to, but its captain refused to slow down or stop until bullets nearly killed his first mate. Then the captain appeared on deck and shouted, "You had better by Christ hurry up. . . . This is a damned outrage. . . . Such god damned bungling I've never seen in my life and I've seen some damned rotten bungling during my time in the Navy." The agency found no liquor but wanted to charge the captain with profanity. The idea was dropped as his company fired him over the much-publicized incident.[19]

Figure 1.2. Cat and Mouse on Rum Row
The presence of the *Gaspé Fisherman*, linked to the Staten Island Fox-Levine gang, was monitored on Rum Row for three years by the Coast Guard. Eventually the rumrunner sank, loaded with champagne, off Nantucket. Courtesy of the National Archives.

Another U.S. ship came under Coast Guard fire while its crew was below deck at dinner. The captain rushed to the deck to protest and a bullet passed inches from his head. He thought he heard laughter from the guardsmen who were a mere fifty yards away. Once safely on shore, the captain filed an official protest. "Is there any law to allow any person to attempt to kill another on the high seas," he asked? Yet another U.S. boat, a yacht, was chased forty miles out by the Coast Guard before being rammed.[20]

Radios, Planes, and Submarines

Rum Row utilized the latest technology. Smugglers used short-wave radios and regular radio frequencies to communicate from Rum Row and had land stations on Long Island, Long Island Sound, Brooklyn, Staten Island, and the Atlantic Highlands in New Jersey. Eventually the Coast Guard created a "crack" radio unit in Manhattan to locate rum stations from Maine to Florida and four patrol boats were assigned to this unit along with competent radio personnel. The destroyers also had radio capability. The purpose of the unit was to intercept, decode, and disseminate information in rum messages. This was necessary because supply ships on Rum Row over the years had been sending coded messages through a commercial radio station to their representatives in Montreal giving the day's liquor sales, daily receipts, quantity of liquor left on board, requests for provisions, and, most importantly, exact locations.

Rum codes used on New York's Rum Row were "more complicated and harder to decipher than any code which was used during the [recent] world war." Elizebeth [sic] Smith Friedman, wife of the U.S. Army's chief cryptologist in World War I and World War II, decoded thousands of rumrunner messages for the Prohibition Bureau and for the Coast Guard before the latter created its own cryptological team. Codes in Chicago and Seattle were not as sophisticated, probably because less was at stake: most smuggling was on the East Coast. In Chicago, specific music played over commercial radio conveyed information to bootleggers. In Seattle, clues were hidden in children's bedtime stories read over the radio by a bootlegger's wife. In the course of radio monitoring of Rum Row, the Coast Guard also learned of the smuggling of Swiss watches, French perfume, contraceptives, narcotics, and aliens.[21]

The Coast Guard was proud of one case related to radio traffic from Rum Row, based on overhearing and decoding the following message: "Man fell overboard from us and drowned. Man belonged to collier [coal ship]. We stopped and searched for him. Found and picked up life buoys that collier through [threw] over. Didn't find man. PNW [supercargo] decided I stop and search for him. They [collier] proceeded." The name and destination of the coal ship, which had picked up liquor on Rum Row, were unknown. The Coast Guard was on alert along the East Coast to search arriving colliers to find one with a missing crewman. One search turned up "a poor hungry-looking scared South Carolina cracker" but no liquor. Then a coal ship arrived in New York with a man missing and liquor stored in its wing tanks. The land station, near Jamaica Bay in Greater New York Bay, received the original message from Rum Row and radioed back, "There is a big row over that man. She was met at Quarantine [off Staten Island] by four cutters. . . . Did you hear the collier [coal ship] radio that news?" The Coast Guard was pleased that smugglers thought the coal ship had leaked the news because the agency did not want rumrunners to know that their code had been broken.[22]

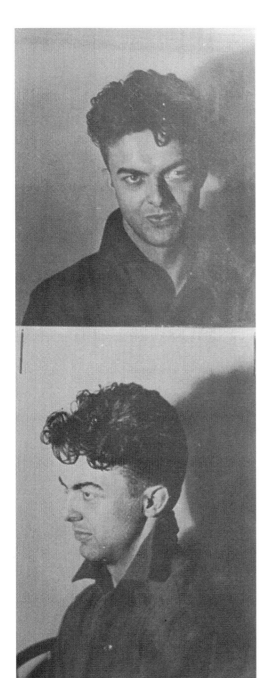

Figure 1.3. Rum Radio
Operator
The Feldman gang, based on
Lower Broadway, operated
in the Chesapeake Bay and
relied on Harwood Park to
make radio contact between
land and sea. When the
entire gang was arrested,
police made these mug shots
of Park, who lived at 4323
40th Street, Long Island
City, New York. Courtesy of
the National Archives.

Early on, the Coast Guard requested a seaplane for use over Rum Row but this request was refused. This gave smugglers a head start in aerial transportation: they used planes to locate supply ships and then notified supply ships and, if radio contact was not possible, dropped messages in bottles to ships below. Smugglers also used planes to locate Coast Guard destroyers. Seaplanes were used to pick up liquor on the Row. One pilot buzzed the Coast Guard below each time he took off. Then his engine failed, his plane was captured, and it was ignominiously towed all the way back to New York harbor. The pilot continued to smuggle afterward, but no longer buzzed the Coast Guard. William Bell Atwater, who gave Franklin D. Roosevelt as a personal reference from Atwater's time as head of U.S. Naval Air forces in Italy during World War I, was charged with stealing a plane from New York's Curtiss Air Field to fetch alcohol from Rum Row. These charges were eventually dropped.[23]

By the end of the 1920s, the Coast Guard seemed to have at least one plane judging from an incident involving a modern, newly built rumrunner out of Nova Scotia. Its captain unwisely bragged to reporters of making many successful liquor hauls to New York City. Not long after this appeared in print, an unidentified airplane circled his ship as it approached Rum Row. Small bombs began dropping on the ship, one down its smoke stack and another on its deck. Then the Coast Guard arrived to escort the ship into a U.S. port where a high-ranking officer came aboard, apologized, saying that the ship had been mistaken for a pirate ship, and advised the captain he was now free to depart.[24]

News of a submarine being used on Rum Row appears to have some substance to it. One smuggler testified in court that he saw a submarine emerge on the Row with a German captain and a French crew. Newspapers in 1924 reported that submarines were smuggling liquor to New Jersey and Cape Cod. An aerial photo, taken by a commercial Manhattan map-making firm that same year, suggested submarines were thirty miles up the Hudson River near Croton Point. (German submarines were kept out of the river during World War I by a steel net strung low across the bottom of the Narrows.) The photo purported to document two submarines below the surface of the Hudson River, each 250 feet long and 600 feet apart. The aerial firm sent the photograph to the U.S. Navy, which had no submarines in the area, and the startling image was given to Coast Guard Intelligence and filed away.[25]

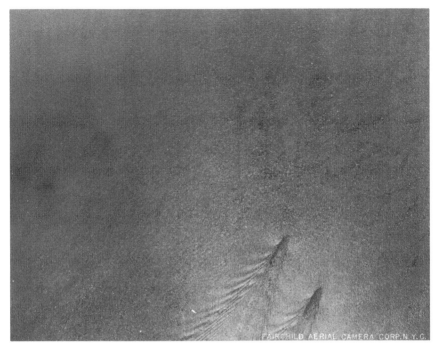

Figure 1.4. Rum Submarines in the Hudson River?
An aerial photograph, taken by a Manhattan map-making firm June 11, 1924, near Croton Point, purports to document two submarines (possibly rumrunners), each about 250 feet long and 600 feet apart, below the surface. Courtesy of the National Archives.

Human Interest

Rum Row had its human side—sometimes sad and sometimes humorous—as well as a technological history. Wives, sisters, mothers, daughters, and sweethearts waited anxiously on shore for their men to return from the Row. A rare private note found aboard one seized vessel demonstrates this: a woman named Ann wrote her lover, "Dearest Don, You do not realize how much you torture me. I lie here worrying myself sick over you." A woman in Little Italy wrote her brother-in-law, jailed for smuggling and requesting her help, that she could do nothing because her own life was in crisis. She wrote, "Do not curse anyone, no one is to blame; fate has persecuted my house," adding, "I am aware of the conditions in which you are placed and am exceedingly sorry." Most rumrunning from shore was done at night to escape detection, leading to many sleepless nights for loved ones at home. Some stayed up all night knitting sweaters to keep their minds occupied. One smuggler's wife awoke suddenly in the middle of the night with a premonition of harm—the police appeared on her doorsteps the next morning to report her husband's death in the night by drowning. A New York bootlegger, in Cuba arranging for liquor shipments, received a letter from his sister apologizing for not packing well for his trip. She wrote, "I got your postal and then was quite sure that your pajamas were left behind. I was awfully sorry but had so many things in my head I forgot to look for them."[26]

Although Rum Row was mainly a male preserve, there were a few women there—as cooks, wives, or guests of the captain. A boatload of Manhattan prostitutes ventured out one summer given the added attraction, besides the sailors, of free liquor and fresh seafood. Women from Long Branch and Asbury Park on the Jersey shore went to Rum Row to "improve their complexions" and get fresh sea air. Two women, who gave their address as a New York hotel, were aboard a yacht seized off Rum Row with liquor. Although its captain and crew were arrested, the women were not arrested as they maintained that they knew nothing about the smuggling. During the trip back to New York City, they stayed near the guardsmen saying they now feared bodily harm from captain and crew.[27]

A singular woman in the history of New York's Rum Row was Gertrude Lythgoe, Scots-American wholesaler employed by London's Haig and MacTavish Scotch Whiskey. She was dubbed "Queen of Rum Row" by the media, because she spent weeks aboard McCoy's ship one summer after male wholesalers in Nassau squeezed her out of that market because her liquor was better. After her liquor was sold, she took a speedboat from Rum Row to Long Island and a taxi to Manhattan and stayed at the Waldorf-Astoria. Eventually, she was recalled to London by her employers who were appalled to learn she had gone directly to Rum Row.[28]

There were African-Americans on Rum Row, usually as sailors. McCoy, in the vernacular of the time, remarked on a "nigger schooner" on Rum Row. Coast Guard records mention stopping one suspected rumrunner and its "colored" captain outward bound from Harlem to the

Figure 1.5. Queen of Rum Row
Gertrude Lythgoe, nominated by the press to be Queen of Rum Row, sold liquor in the Bahamas to U.S. smugglers. She sailed one summer with the well-known rum smuggler Captain Bill McCoy. Courtesy of the Flat Hammock Press.

British West Indies. When this ship was stopped, no liquor was found. Amos Lover, an African-American FBI informant, sailed on a rumrunner to Nova Scotia and passed back information about a loaded rumrunner bound for New York City. A Nassau policeman named Pindar, "the dusty one," was hijacked on a rum ship leaving the Bahamas and forced to work until it reached New York. There he was released and told to go back home, but instead went to the authorities and testified against the gang.[29]

The names of a few rumrunners reflected their owners' sense of humor. The *Alpaca* reputedly belonged to Chicago's Al Capone. A "Honduran" rumrunner was named the *Al Smith* to honor the Governor of New York, the only wet candidate for president in the 1920s. *Woodgod's* name referred to alcohol. The *Whatzis* and *Notus* proclaimed innocence. The *Mazel Tov* was Yiddish for a celebratory toast. *Mary Mother Elizabeth* honored a Roman Catholic Mother Superior in Hempstead, Long Island.

Coast Guard destroyers, cruisers, cutters, and patrol boats had names such as *Hudson* and *Manhattan*. Many were named for Native-American

Figure 1.6. Capone's Namesake
The Coast Guard believed that the *Alpaca*, a Nova Scotia ship, shown here alongside a Norwegian supply ship, belonged to Al Capone and its name meant "Al packs [it]." Courtesy of the National Archives.

tribes, for example *Algonquin, Haida, Modoc, Mojav, Ossipee, Seminole, Seneca, Tampa, Tuscarora, Unalga, Yamacraw, Acushnet, Apache,* and *Cahokia*.

Vinnie Higgins, an Irish-American gangster from Brooklyn, delighted in being witty. He was in a speedboat idling adjacent to a known rumrunner outside New York harbor, but insisted to arresting officers that he was innocently fishing although no fishing gear was aboard. He later maintained to reporters that it was purely accidental he was found fishing near the *Whichone* as he could have been fishing near *any* one.

2

ALONG THE SHORE

Liquor shipped to Rum Row from Nassau, Europe, Canada, or Cuba was worthless unless it could be smuggled to shore. The coasts of Long Island and Northern New Jersey were closer and/or easier to access than Manhattan.

South Coast of Long Island

Long Island's 118 miles of inlets, harbors, rivers, and estates were used by liquor smugglers during Prohibition. Montauk Point, on the easternmost end, was a paradise for smugglers given its extensive coastal area and proximity to Rum Row. Smugglers were recruited locally for contact boats and ships because they knew the channels, marshes, and beaches better than anyone and usually had fast engines to outrun the Coast Guard. In a few cases, smugglers used noxious smokescreens. When liquor reached shore, it was hauled by truck to New York City in convoys, which usually traveled the local highways and streets late at night, with armed gangsters "riding shotgun" to prevent hijacking by rival gangs. Local police were often well paid to look the other way and/or even to stand guard near the beaches and direct civilian traffic away. In a few cases, police escorted convoys back to New York City, although sometimes the escorts were gangsters dressed in police uniform.

Residents living near Long Island beaches and inlets sometimes heard gunfire in the night and did not know who was firing. It could have

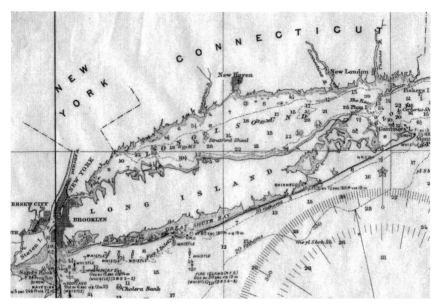

Figure 2.1. Nautical Chart of Long Island
Long Island, given its proximity to Rum Row, provided smugglers with many landing sites. Courtesy of the National Archives.

been either the Coast Guard or smugglers. The first Coast Guard fatality in the Rum War was Carl Gustavson off Montauk. His death was unusual because smugglers, although feeling free to shoot at rivals, rarely returned government gunfire as the penalty, if caught, was severe. They were employed to deliver liquor and not kill or die for it. Rum captains sometimes deliberately steered close to populated shorelines counting on the Coast Guard policy of not firing near beach homes, although residents along Pleasure Beach near Mattituck Inlet reported hearing gunfire during one chase. If smugglers were hauling a heavy load preventing escape during a chase, they might toss cases of liquor overboard so they could go faster and return later to pick up the floating liquor cases. Or they hired professional divers to bring cases to the surface. Several rumrunning boats and ships were shipwrecked off Montauk Point. (One was not wrecked, according to its owner, but boxed in and rammed by the Coast Guard.) Another boat went aground on Shagwong Reef trying to slip into Fort Pond Bay after being trailed for a week by the Coast Guard. A third, while taking twenty-five rounds of gunfire, managed to destroy or toss all the liquor overboard prior to its capture. A fourth was seized after catching fire and being abandoned near that reef.[1]

A former American Red Cross yacht from World War I, belonging to Arthur Deery of 527 Fifth Avenue in Manhattan, was seized less than two miles off Montauk Point on its return from Rum Row despite an offer of a $10,000 bribe. John Hayes of Montauk was its captain. The yacht had been trailed seventy miles by the Coast Guard for ten hours and closely "shadowed" for the last twenty-seven miles. The main cause for suspicion of smuggling was its painted waterline, which was flush with the water suggesting a heavy load. (In fact it was carrying four thousand cases of whiskey.) The yacht may have been headed for the Benson Estate on Montauk for storage, where the caretaker reputedly was paid a dollar a case, or perhaps the load was to be hauled to the Wyandannee Hotel or to the Yacht Club docks of Fort Pond Bay.[2]

Gardiners Bay, separating Long Island's South and North Forks, saw its share of smuggling. Two residents of nearby Greenport, a Dr. Johnson and a Robert Clark, each owned a rumrunner. Johnson kept his right at the dock, while Clark's was seized off Montauk with five hundred cases of liquor. Claudio's Restaurant in Greenport, built on stilts out over the water, had a trapdoor where liquor cases could be passed up for temporary storage before being hauled to New York City. The proprietor refused to participate in smuggling after a driver was killed in 1926. A "fishing launch," with a sharp hull and a powerful motor, was seized off Culloden Point on the South Fork: an incredulous official later asked, "What fish needs 800 horsepower to catch it?"[3]

Occasionally smugglers competed with local residents for liquor tossed overboard or lost in shipwrecks near the coast. A Nova Scotia trawler, owned by a Brooklyn man, went aground one night near Black Fish Rock in Montauk, and hundreds of bags of liquor bottles were jettisoned prior to the wreck. Among the first to arrive at the beach were several couples returning at three in the morning from a Masonic dinner at the Fort Pond Bay Restaurant. When they slowed their car to see what was going on, shots were fired and guardsmen surrounded their car. Later a guardsman, searching the beach in the dark, found one "native lying on the sand, unconscious, and covered with coats, who, the natives said, had passed out from drinking too much of the contraband liquor." At dawn, Lennan Edwards, William Young, Stephen L. Morley, and Benjamin H. Barnes arrived at the beach with eel spears, clam rakes, and nets to toss into the surf to salvage the liquor. They were halted by gun volleys to the beach from two newly arrived Coast Guard boats from New London. When East Hampton deputy sheriffs Jensen and Mortiana arrived, they complained to the Coast Guard about the firing on the beach and were assured no shots were aimed at people and none had landed close to anyone. Mason James J. Hildreth later swore out a John Doe Warrant of *felonious assault* [intended to harm] on himself, Mrs. Hildreth, Mr. and Mrs. William Young, Mr. and Mrs. Fred Scribner, Mr. and Mrs. Benjamin Barnes, Stephen L. Marley, Cecil Wyer, Richard Bennett, Fred Budd, and Romeo Rozzi. Suffolk County District Attorney Alexander G. Blue told reporters, "I am going to get to the bottom of this and I am going to stop this practice of indiscriminate shooting by Coast Guardsmen at citizens of eastern Long Island."[4]

T. Budd King's and Emerson Tabor's Hampton syndicate brought in ten thousand cases a month near Montauk and the Hamptons at the end of Prohibition. The gang received valuable radio intelligence from an ex–Coast Guardsman on the whereabouts of honest Coast Guard patrols in the area. The police in the Hamptons were paid to look the other way. King and Tabor kept money in the East Hampton Bank vault. One of their operations was discovered on a South Hampton beach by guardsmen on beach patrol. They observed forty longshoremen milling about at night with three trucks parked behind the dunes and three horse-drawn wagons right on the beach near the surf. One man, holding a red lantern and signaling to a ship three hundred yards offshore, extinguished the lantern when the Coast Guard arrived. A guardsman relit it and decoyed a dory from the ship to the beach where it and the liquor, as evidence of smuggling, were seized. This King/Tabor gang was probably also involved with the "British" ship seized off East Hampton where the entire crew avoided capture by diving overboard and swimming two hundred yards to shore. Daniel Grimshaw, an oysterman who had been a guardsman before Prohibition, was captured because his boat was alongside the abandoned ship. He admitted being paid a thousand dollars a trip for smuggling to shore and insisted that those who fled were not Hampton locals as he knew none of them.[5]

Fire Island and Great South Bay were also popular with smugglers. Patchogue, east of Bay Shore, had a rum radio station on the Leitches Estate used by men described by the Coast Guard as a "gang of Jews." Bay Shore, located on the mainland opposite Fire Island, was home to John Holving who lived adjacent to the beach. Once, he looked outside and saw guardsmen on beach patrol observing dories pulled up on the sand and many footprints leading to his door. He went outside to offer them a bribe, promising to rake away the incriminating tracks, and said he was hard up due to the Depression and earned money storing smuggled liquor. A speedboat, chased one winter off Bay Shore by the Coast Guard, dumped liquor cases onto ice floes for later pickup. The Coast Guard discovered this same boat later, in an Islip shipyard with telltale ice cuts to its bow.[6]

Several Bay Shore residents were "notorious" bootleggers, including the brothers George and William Murdock, Ed Baker, Archie Scarborough, and William Ryan. The brothers were captured aboard R. W. Alcock's fishing trawler along with liquor under his shrimp cargo. His lawyer sought to reassure the Coast Guard that his client had been tempted into rumrunning but intended henceforth to be a legitimate fisherman. "While he may be tempted in the same manner as before and may yield," his lawyer explained, this should not be used to deny him a license as fishing was his livelihood. On the other hand, the lawyer suggested the Coast Guard would be well-advised to keep the shrimp boat under "rigid scrutiny." As for Ed Baker and Archie Scarborough, they knew every inch of the local bays and marshes and could muffle their engines and be hard to find on dark, foggy nights. The two men, along with William Ryan, hung out at Ray's Fish Dock near Fire Island Inlet. A passerby near Maple Avenue's dock in Bay Shore heard moans coming from a boat owned by Ryan. They came from Anthony Sczerbinsh, injured and abandoned in it. He was transported to the local hospital where he died. He had been crushed between two boats at sea, probably when liquor was being transported from one to the other, and left behind in the speedboat when it reached the dock.[7]

Bay Shore's Archie M. Glock owned a steam trawler captained by Norwegian-American "Big Bill" Apsch of Islip, known in the area as a successful smuggler. Captain Apsch and Thomas Shea of Brooklyn were on a trawler anchored in Great South Bay when two Prohibition agents rowed out to their boat. Apsch deliberately dove into the water and upset the row boat before swimming to shore a mile away, but Shea used a life preserver to save the agent, who could not swim and was floundering in the water. State troopers later found Apsch's body in the marsh near Timber Point Golf Club in Great River, west of Islip. He was survived by a wife and two young children. His wife said she had awakened in the middle of the night with a premonition of disaster.[8]

In the early days of Prohibition, when Rum Row was three miles out, a Dutch ship was seized off Fire Island carrying champagne for the Christmas season. The U.S. Circuit Court ordered the sloop returned as no evidence was presented that the liquor was intended for the United States. When the case was retried, proof was presented that the ship landed on Cholera Banks, ten miles south of Jones Inlet, and that its supercargo had been in New York City taking orders for the liquor. In another instance off Fire Island, sailors aboard a rum ship anchored there were near mutiny when the bootleg gang, which owned the liquor, removed it too slowly because they were partying on Broadway between trips and oblivious to the sailors' deteriorating food situation. In a third case, a contact boat was seized off Fire Island after the captain had already made forty successful trips into New York harbor, possible, he claimed, because a patrol boat was particularly "friendly."[9]

Rudolph Wylk, 8 Maple Street, was implicated in 1922 in an embezzlement of the First National Bank of Rockville Center, ostensibly for the purpose of funding his bootleg operations. He eventually became the main smuggler in the area, owning and operating ships landing in Jones and Debs Inlets and in a fifteen-mile radius of the Fire Island Lightship. One of his aliases was Charles Friedman, a Rockville resident listed as an owner of two ships and a director of Central Import and Export Company Ltd. of St. John's, Newfoundland. One of Wylk's ships was the *Mary Mother Elizabeth* named to honor a friend who was the Mother Superior at Mercy Hospital in Hempstead. His gang used the Dietz Estate in Hempstead where Elias Garduci was caretaker. A Catholic sisterhood, possibly the same one to which the Mother Superior belonged, bought the site for a future convent and government agents were stymied. They wanted to search the estate but worried this might violate the constitutional separation of church and state. Wylk's ships used ship-to-shore radio and his first land station was in a Long Beach hotel until management learned about this and insisted that it be removed. It was relocated to an apartment or home in Freeport.[10]

Peter Blohm of Brooklyn captained several of Wylk's ships. Once after being captured, Blohm confessed to the Coast Guard that he and his associates "were directed by the liquor interests on shore to operate regardless of the number of boats caught by the Coast Guard." He said the U.S. Commissioner at New London was a friend and, with the services of syndicate lawyer Louis Halle, "they had little to fear." But Blohm had a healthy respect for the ocean after one of his ships sank in a winter storm off Long Island, and sailors Chester Carman, Arthur

Langdon, and Michael Cabinoff drowned. Blohm survived by swimming two miles to shore in icy water with thirty-foot swells and fifty mile per hour winds. Mrs. Cabinoff, disappointed in collecting survivor's insurance money from Wylk, tipped the Nassau County police on his whereabouts. Wylk was arrested, despite offering ten thousand dollars as a bribe to the arresting officer.[11]

Philip Maresca of nearby Freeport was small fish compared to Wylk and Blohm. Maresca owned a single scallop fishing boat seized on Rum Row while it was loading up with liquor. The Coast Guard towed it back to shore, but it sank during the tow. Maresca maintained that it would not have sunk if the Coast Guard had not been using it as target practice. When a fishing boat suspected as a rumrunner was seized in neighboring Freeport, owner John Anderson admitted it was his, but he insisted it had been stolen and used by smugglers without his knowledge. Although his story sounded "fishy," the Coast Guard returned it to him. In the final month of Prohibition in 1933, rumrunners abandoned a boat in the Freeport canal covering its name and homeport with a blanket. It was seized along with the liquor still on it.[12]

Long Beach, west of Fire Island, had a smuggling gang as important as Wylk's in Great South Bay. This was the Frankel-Barbarie-Grossman syndicate protected by law enforcement according to an informer. He explained to the Department of Justice, "Long Beach police stand guard along the ocean while boats are unloaded between three and four o'clock in the morning. Anyone passing [by] is not allowed within a block of the ocean by the motorcycle police. Too much money being divided locally for any results." If the police in Long Beach were on the take, private citizens were not. Two stepped up to the plate during a spring beauty pageant on the boardwalk. The pageant crowd heard shots and looked out to see the Coast Guard chasing a speedboat into shallow water. Then smugglers cut their engine, escaped into a dory, and rowed to the beach planning to disappear into the crowd. But they were foiled by detective Thomas Moore and hotel auditor Herman Charlsky who stepped out of the crowd, tackled them, and made a citizens' arrest.[13]

Long Island Sound

In the winter or during foul weather on Rum Row, smugglers from Canada preferred to skirt the New England coast south to Long Island Sound, the body of water separating the northern shore of Long Island

and the state of Connecticut. Rum radio stations in New Bedford, Massachusetts, Saybrook, Connecticut, and on Montauk Point, guided such boats to Manhattan. Once they reached the western end of the Sound, they could proceed through the waters of Hell Gate and go south on the East River or north through the Spuyten Duyval Canal to the Hudson River. Or they could land on either side of the Sound and have the liquor taken by truck to the city.

Orient Point, on Long Island's North Fork guarding the entrance to the Sound, was a frequent landing spot. The chief of the Destroyer Force in New London, across the Sound, once asked for and received permission to borrow a plane and to hire a pilot to fly low over Orient Point where he suspected liquor was being landed. He and the pilot looked down and saw hundreds of people carrying liquor sacks and cases up the beach and through dunes and beach grass. He said it looked like they were ants carrying eggs. Authorities seized New Yorker A. C. Drew's yacht near Little Gull Light. It was designed for rumrunning with metal sheeting around its pilot house to deflect bullets and an interior gutted to permit large cargoes. Another yacht, with liquor hidden under a concrete deck and steel plates, had forged documents aboard using legitimate seals from the New York Customs Office. As a U.S. vice-consul in Nassau had voyaged on the yacht a few weeks earlier from Nassau to New York, the forms and seals were presumed to have been stolen at that time. After this discovery an order went out, many years into Prohibition, to lock up all forms and seals.[14]

A big deterrent to smugglers using Long Island Sound should have been the main Coast Guard base in New London. But Otto Lindberg's Castle Inn at Cornfield Point, Old Saybrook, just to the west, had a radio tower to monitor Coast Guard movements and his son-in-law, August C. Strusholm, owned several rumrunners. Even New London itself was not off-limits to smugglers. During a New Year's Eve party at Mrs. Ruth Cunningham's home, twenty-four guardsmen drank liquor confiscated earlier by the Coast Guard. When this was discovered, the men were placed under general court martial, and a surprise search was ordered for the same batch of seized liquor aboard destroyers on Rum Row. Smugglers also relied on signals from a corrupt Coast Guard boat operating off Block Island: one flashing light meant "Stop Loading," two indicated "Coast Clear," and three warned "Beat it!"[15]

A Newfoundland fishing boat with 1,355 barrels of herring aboard was stopped several times in the Sound. Each time the captain swore there was no liquor aboard and requested that any search be done once he reached Manhattan. He didn't want the herring to spoil. The Coast Guard agreed and discovered that he was telling the truth, although earlier he had been caught smuggling liquor. When one known rum ship evaded capture in the Sound, reporters asked W. V. E. Jacobs, Coast Guard Commander of the New York Division, for an explanation. The Commander said, "She gave us the slip in the Sound and the East River. Whether she unloaded any liquor is problematical because our boats never caught sight of her coming or going." While experienced smugglers evaded capture, others were not so fortunate. Mr. and Mrs. C. H. Goddard of Manhattan, when they

Figure 2.2. Halted in Long Island Sound
The fishing vessel *George Cochran* (far left), a known rumrunner from Newfoundland, was stopped and threatened with a search off the New England coast and again in Long Island Sound. It was not searched until docking in Manhattan because its captain successfully argued that the herring aboard would spoil if not gotten quickly to market. The ensuing search found only herring aboard. Courtesy of the National Archives.

took a summer cruise on their houseboat in the Sound, were stopped and their boat searched. Twenty-three liquor bottles were found. The Goddards, their guests, servants, and crew were arrested and imprisoned aboard the houseboat as it was towed back to Manhattan.[16]

Huntington Bay was a haven for smugglers. One winter an Italian schooner, owned by Antonio Romano Sr., and carrying liquor purchased in Cuba for G. Venza in Manhattan's Little Italy, was seized in the bay. The owner's sons, Captain Michelangelo Romano, twenty-seven, and second mate Antonio Romano, twenty-five, were arrested along with first-mate Antonio Gallo, forty-five. All were from Castellammare del Golfo, Sicily. No liquor was aboard although corks were strewn everywhere about the deck, and the manifest showed eight thousand cases of whiskey and champagne had been picked up earlier in Havana. Two revolvers, an automatic pistol, and a shot gun were seized along with several personal and business letters from the captain's cabin. The Coast Guard believed the Brooklyn District Attorney's Office was uninterested in pursuing the case because neither Venza nor the captain's uncle, a Long Island lace maker, were questioned after visiting the three jailed smugglers.[17]

The letters revealed that Venza hired the Romanos and advised them to deal respectfully with H. J. Levin, his contact in Havana. Their father warned them not to get involved in smuggling liquor: "Frankly I tell you, if [you receive this] in time, I would advise against it." Their uncle wrote, "I have no money to lend, especially not knowing how it will be repaid. . . . I hear that you have found a cargo for this bay; let us hope that we will have a little gain." The Sicilians were found guilty based solely on these letters as no physical evidence of smuggling existed except for the corks on deck. Neither captain nor mates admitted guilt. An appeals court reversed the convictions noting that the corks could have come from liquor discharged legally on Rum Row as it was "not a crime to sell or deliver intoxicating liquors on the high seas," and observing that "unfair inferences were made from letters which themselves could have been fictitious."[18]

A fireman aboard a coal ship testified that his ship picked up liquor in Nova Scotia and delivered it to Oyster Bay. Initially he had been intimidated into going along by armed smugglers who boarded in Boston, and then seduced with the promise of a $100 bonus, which he never received. When a rum schooner went aground at night off Bayville, police and guardsmen kept salvagers and bootleggers off the beach

while the Coast Guard offshore raked the beach with its searchlight.
A Manhattan writer, renting an estate in Oyster Bay, departed for a
Christmas trip. Thousands of cases of champagne were delivered to the
estate while he was gone. Neighbors were each given a case in return for
their silence. The writer returned to find smugglers sleeping in his house,
wearing his clothes, using his phone, and charging groceries at the local
store in his name. After he chased them away, he bought two pistols
and grimly settled into enjoying his remaining months on the estate.[19]

Smugglers also liked Long Island Sound because its northern shoreline belonged to Connecticut, which, along with Rhode Island, never
ratified the 18th Amendment. Judges there were friendly to smugglers.
Once a rumrunner was chased and fired on off Black Point, near Nian-
tic, and a stray bullet entered a vacant beach home belonging to T. M.
Taft of Williams Street, Manhattan. Adjacent to this vacation home
was one belonging to a New York Supreme Court judge and his wife
who were furious and demanded an official investigation. Subsequently,
the Coast Guard determined that the shot entered the vacant home,
passed three feet in from its left-hand corner, streaked along a piece of
board, damaged the lower part of a circular picture about four feet in
diameter, and exited the back wall while damaging three shingles. The
Coast Guard offered to pay damages. In another instance, a shot entered
a beach house at Sakonnet, Rhode Island. Coast Guard Intelligence
advised that seized vessels not be hauled into that state again because
prosecuting such cases in Rhode Island was "like playing baseball in the
other fellow's backyard."[20]

In Bridgeport, Connecticut, Charles Samuelson was critically
wounded when the Coast Guard opened fire on his boat. He was rushed
to a nearby hospital where a local attorney requested, on behalf of an
unidentified New Yorker, that no expense be spared in saving Samuelson's life.[21]

Forty longshoremen from New York were arrested at the Stamford
Mason Supply Company docks in Connecticut after Annie Hill, a widow
caretaker living near the company pier, noticed them one night and
phoned authorities. They had been unloading liquor hidden beneath
stone slabs transported from Maine. Mrs. Hill was particularly worried
because her teenage son had volunteered to work with the smugglers to
earn some money. Louis Pope, prominent in Westchester County, Isadore
Skulky of Port Chester, Jack Saunders of 123 Herzel Street, Brooklyn,
and Harry Gordan of New York's Hotel Forrest, New York, were in a

car parked near the dock, overseeing the unloading, and were arrested. (Mrs. Hill's son was not arrested.) Near Greenwich, a schooner smuggling twenty thousand cases of liquor was seized. The informer in that case described the captain as the son of Archie Publicover of Staten Island, "a nice, pleasant young chap and would not, perhaps, become involved in anything irregular were it not for the fact that he has to carry out the wishes of his father." Port Chester, New York, on the western end of the Sound adjacent to the Connecticut line, was home to Emil Wormser's smuggling syndicate with assets of ten million dollars.[22]

An odd tale of smuggling connected with Long Island Sound took place hundreds of miles away in the Canadian Maritime Provinces. There Argus Swope Wagner Jr., twenty-two, claiming to be from New Sound, Long Island, sailed a yacht from a Massachusetts harbor to Halifax. There he caused a local sensation trying to elope with an underage girl, but the ceremony was stopped in time by her mother. Wagner was described as "a well-dressed, rather prepossessing young man of Scandinavian heritage." A few days later the couple married with the mother's blessing, but the groom was arrested before they could sail off on their honeymoon. The authorities believed he had stolen the yacht and was an American bootlegger.[23]

The Coasts of Brooklyn and Staten Island

Coney Island, Sheepshead Bay, Gravesend Bay, Jamaica Bay, and Rockaway are on the southwestern shore of Long Island. These sites were popular with rumrunners because liquor landed there could easily be trucked to Manhattan across the Brooklyn Bridge.

Despite the fact the Coast Guard had its first radio station at the Rockaway Point Coast Guard Base, the Rockaways remained popular with smugglers. One aggrieved smuggler informed on a boat on East Rockaway Inlet because the gang owning the ship had done him "a pretty mean trick." He gave names of individuals, radio codes, and a hand-drawn map showing a radio beacon located on Montauk Point and advised the Coast Guard that smugglers "always unload during the dark of the moon." Customs searched an ocean liner anchored off Rockaway and found six hundred liquor bottles in one water tank. (The same ship docked in Manhattan after another trip, and agents fought a fist and gun battle with twenty-five longshoremen before seizing one thousand bottles of wine.) Mr. and Mrs. Edward Green of New York City chartered a yacht, which was seized with hundreds of cases of liquor off Rockaway Point. The same yacht was stranded earlier on a Cape Cod beach, rescued by the Coast Guard, and kept under surveillance because those aboard were not yachtsmen and the engineer was a known bootlegger. Another time the Coast Guard chased a boat off Rockaway firing 120 rounds from Lewis M. machine guns and 220 rounds from a Thompson submachine gun, scoring 46 hits and sending up 12 flares. Despite this bombardment, the rumrunner escaped after releasing an "obnoxious" smokescreen. When it was discovered later in dry dock, it was seized before it could be relaunched.[24]

Sheepshead Bay had smugglers. During one chase, with ninety rounds of Thompson submachine fire from the Coast Guard, the rum-runner caught fire and sank, and the smugglers fled. The officer in charge commended his marksman for accuracy as, "Any nervousness or miscalculation on his part would have resulted in the loss of lives." Another yacht was chased in Sheepshead Bay and shot at twenty-two times, and a fishing vessel with a false bottom was seized off the Bay.[25]

The Coast Guard routinely inspected Gravesend Bay each night observing which boats were missing and probably running in liquor. The first smuggler ever killed by U.S. Customs was in this bay in 1922. After a crewman on another rumrunner was wounded in the head during a shooting in the bay, the boat owner had the deckhouse covered with armor. This did not help as a second crewman was later injured when a bullet passed through the window of the pilot house. Over a two-year span, that particular boat was seized five times including in Great South Bay and Delaware Bay.[26]

Brooklyn's smuggling syndicate was extensive and tough. Before Prohibition, gangster Frankie Yale (Iole), an Italian-American who operated the Harvard Inn, a dance house/brothel on Coney Island, employed young Al Capone as a bouncer. Yale's friend, Johnny Torrio, and Capone moved to Chicago before Prohibition. In the early 1920s, Yale handled liquor smuggled ashore to Brooklyn including some intended for Chicago. Suspected in the assassinations of two of Capone's rivals in Chicago, Yale was also known for violence in New York City. His Brooklyn syndicate was probably responsible for the murder of Isadore Dunsky, whose body was buried in Spermacetti Cove on Sandy Hook. Yale was eventually murdered by hit men from Chicago after being suspected of double-crossing Capone over liquor shipments.[27]

Coney Island's Wheeler's Shipyard retrofitted local boats and tugs for the smuggling trade, making them faster to avoid capture by the Coast Guard. Many Brooklyn-owned smuggling boats and ships had a violent history. Barney Kaufman's superfast boat, "the pride of the rumrunners," was seized off Martha's Vineyard and two crewmen were wounded by gunfire. Three boats belonging to John McCambridge, of Kent Street in Brooklyn, sank at sea with great loss of lives. When John Stack's yacht was seized off Block Island, three crewmen were injured by gunfire, one badly. (Before Prohibition, Stack's yacht, owned by Gale Borden of Borden's Milk Company, was one of the fastest yachts in the New York area.) Nicholas Entenza, a Cuban national living in New York, fronted as owner for a yacht actually owned by a Brooklyn man. This yacht evaded capture for a long time because of its legitimate foreign registration.[28]

Cecil Mollineaux, alias Charles Mollineaux, alias Charles Martin, alias "Sparky," and Malcolm MacMasters, alias Fred Baker, operated a rum radio station in Brooklyn at #51–53 V Avenue. This station came to light when the Coast Guard decoded messages from it to a ship on the water. The initial finding was slightly off and a neighboring home was raided before the agents realized their mistake and went back over the roof and down a fire escape into the correct house. The officer in charge hoped someone, more aware of laws relating to radio than the typical district attorney, would be assigned to the case. The officer thought such attorneys were unfamiliar with radio technology, considering radio "one of life's sweet mysteries."[29]

On first glance, Staten Island was central to Prohibition enforcement at sea. Six Coast Guard destroyers, which patrolled Rum Row, were located here. The island also had a housing development called Prohibition Park, its streets named for politicians and leaders favoring the 18th Amendment. Despite destroyers and street names, the island was a smugglers' haven. The Staten Island Shipbuilding Company retrofitted tugs and boats for the smuggling business. The Fox-Levine smuggling syndicate, based on Staten Island, had an office in lower Manhattan, a rum station in Grant City, and another one on the New England coast. Max Fox, whom Coast Guard records referred to as the "little Jew," owned several rum ships and tugs, which were managed by John (Bert) Crabbitt of New York City. United States Naval Reserve Captain Eugene Edgar Merrill, whose rum alias was "Captain Wilson," lived in Port Richmond. Staten Island was also home to the Marine Hospital, which treated both guardsmen and smugglers wounded in the Rum Wars.[30]

Accounts of rum ships off Staten Island suggest that enforcement there was lax despite the presence of the Coast Guard. For example, despite three hundred shots fired at one rum boat, it escaped in dark and hazy weather. In another instance, a rum captain escaped by jumping onto a wharf as his trawler was towed through the Narrows. In still another instance, an entire crew escaped in dories while their ship was being towed and, according to a district attorney, this was the third time within a few months that an entire crew escaped in this fashion.[31]

Northern New Jersey Coast

Sea Girt, Sea Bright, Port Monmouth, Perth Amboy, Atlantic Highlands, Raritan Bay, and Sandy Hook were popular New Jersey landing sites for liquor bound for Manhattan. A cottage in the area, once owned by Oscar Hammerstein, was called the "Estate" by smugglers using it as a rum radio station.

While cruising off Roamers Shoals Light near Raritan Bay, the Coast Guard chased a high-powered motor boat near Sandy Hook for half an hour with 150 shots fired by both smugglers and guardsmen. Two bullets killed Captain Antonio Pietro of Astoria. His crew included two Manhattan sailors, two from Brooklyn, and one from the Bronx. In another deadly instance, the Coast Guard shot and killed Gerard Kadenbach, son of the owner of Highlands' hardware store. After a rumrunner was chased and fired on near Sandy Hook, an unnamed smuggler was lost overboard, sixteen others were rescued, and eighteen hundred cases of champagne went down with the sinking ship. Another time, a New York corporation's tug and barge were seized off Sea Girt with liquor stored in the "oil" tanks.[32]

Also off Sea Girt, the Coast Guard chased and fired on four men in a speedboat and then rescued them when their boat sank. The appearance of the four aroused suspicion but, as they had no liquor in their possession, they were released. There was no camera to photograph them, so detailed written descriptions were recorded. One twenty-nine-year-old man had a "round face, tough expression, ruddy complexion, dark brown hair, blue flannel shirt, dark blue sweater, blue serge trousers, and no hat." A twenty-one-year-old had a "ruddy complexion, high cheek bones, pleasant expression, dark brown hair tinged with grey, cambric shirt, dark greasy trousers, and no hat." The third man, forty, had a "sallow complexion, drawn and wrinkled features, long thin nose, light curly brown hair, blue jumper, grey cambric shirt, dark trousers." The fourth was a Brooklyn man with a "ruddy complexion, full face, prominent scar across nose, high forehead, dark hair, faded khakis, dark trousers, and no hat." The guardsman writing these descriptions added to his notes, "I understand these men frequent a liquor saloon run by a widow named Toohey at Belford, New Jersey, and are classed as pretty tough characters." The four actually were pirates returning from a successful period on Rum Row hijacking liquor from a French ship onto a boat belonging to their gang, but the Coast Guard did not know that. They may also have been among the twenty-four armed men who pirated a rum schooner off Sea Bright when the legal limit was only three miles.[33]

New Jersey Coast Guard stations had a mixed record in Prohibition. An officer at the Sandy Hook station would misdirect his men when notified by smugglers of times and places of landings. John Campbell, owner of a "British" schooner on Rum Row, was convicted of conspiracy with guardsmen at another New Jersey station. When one of Campbell's ships was pirated, Harry Henderson was shot in retaliation. Liquor syndicates off the Atlantic Highlands also smuggled narcotics, which were made illegal in 1922. Many who opposed Prohibition did not oppose the new ban on narcotics. "When it comes to dope, I do [care] and therefore believe it is my duty to report same," one informer wrote.[34]

Ralph Bitters of the Highlands, wounded in a gang war between locals and Newark gangsters, owned an armored speedboat. It came to the attention of the Coast Guard after it was stopped and the guardsman who boarded it "brutally assaulted," before the speedboat took off and disappeared. The Coast Guard was determined to find Bitters, searching the bays and waterways of Staten Island and Sandy Hook to no avail. When the speedboat was sighted near a Honduran schooner off the Jersey coast, the Coast Guard boarded both the speedboat and the schooner and confiscated pictures the captain had taken during a recent vacation in Cuba. Among the photographs were some believed to be of Ralph Bitters, supercargo on the same ship. The ship was released because its papers were in order.[35]

Blockades Drive New Yorkers Farther South

Eight years into Prohibition, Lieutenant Commander Charles S. Root observed that New York City remained the nation's largest liquor mar-

Figure 2.3. Bootleggers at Leisure
This unique snapshot shows New Jersey bootlegger Ralph Bitters, Captain Jack
Duran, and a friend on a beach, probably in Cuba but perhaps in New Jersey.
The picture was developed from a roll of film seized in a search at sea of the
Julito. Courtesy of the National Archives.

ket, a strong temptation for rumrunners. "It seems trite to say that if
the entrance to New York harbor were blockaded, the problem [smug-
gling] would be solved." But it was impolitic to blockade the nation's
largest port. During short-lived semi-blockades, which lasted for weeks
at a time, smugglers diverted liquor to Long Island Sound, Northern
New Jersey, and, if necessary, farther south.[36]

Just before New Year's Eve, a tug and a coal barge off Barnegat
Lighthouse, midway on the Jersey coast, were seized because speedboats and a foreign rumrunner were seen to be "working the barge."
When guardsmen boarded, a single man was at the wheel and they
found twenty-three more crewmen or longshoremen from New York
hiding among the liquor. All were drunk on champagne. The sailors
or longshoremen insisted they had been captured because they were
"singing lustily" and could be heard in a patrol boat across the water.
The president of the company owning the barge and tug, in business

fifty years, insisted that his company was innocent, wished "to go on record that we are not in the rum business," and maintained his barge and tug had been hijacked. Suffering financially from the seizure, he requested Coast Guard protection for his other barges against hijackers. Instead, the agency suggested he improve supervision of his personnel.[37]

When a yacht owned by Samuel Gottlieb from the Bronx was seized off the Delaware Capes, Judge J. Dickinson, for the District Court in East Pennsylvania, noted a "five minute acquaintance" with the yacht would convince anyone that it was "designed, built, rigged, and fully maintained and equipped to engage in trade, if it may be called such, of violating the National Prohibition Law." But, lacking legal proof, he was obliged to rule that the yacht "was not a rum runner although everyone knows she was." Charles and Red Agnew were rumored to be working closely with New York smugglers near Maryland's Ocean City.[38]

The New York gang of Benjamin Feldman, president of Bango Shipping and Chartering on lower Broadway in Manhattan, operated in Chesapeake Bay. Gang members were captured in Maryland waiting for liquor to be landed and released as no liquor was seized. Later two speedboats were captured off Wingate's Point and Taylor's Island, and this time liquor was seized. Two captains, two crews, several longshoremen, a radio man, and Feldman were arrested. Also in Chesapeake Bay, John Gross, "colored" master of a schooner, admitted that he had obtained liquor from a steamer to load onto a barge which carried liquor for New York City through the Chesapeake and Delaware Canal. The barge was seized in the canal.[39]

A four-masted rum schooner from Nova Scotia with liquor for New York City, sailed into Delaware Bay and up the river to Wilmington and later into Chesapeake Bay to Baltimore. Amos Lover, an African-American informer operating undercover in Halifax, alerted the Coast Guard that a rumrunner would assume the name of a five-masted schooner expected to make legitimate deliveries to those cities. Despite this warning, the rumrunner delivered the liquor unmolested: guardsmen in Delaware Bay and Chesapeake Bay were unable to distinguish four masts from five, or had been bribed. On shore, the liquor was then transferred to Pennsylvania Railroad freight cars, which were sealed and labeled "canned tomatoes" bound for the Bonafide Grocery Store, Fourth Street in Brooklyn. When the train reached Jersey City, these freight cars were detached, placed on barges, and floated across Upper New York Bay to Brooklyn under the noses of the Marine police, Cus-

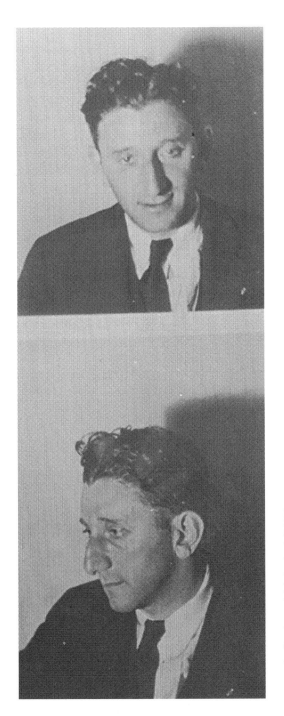

Figure 2.4. Boss of a Manhattan Bootleg Gang These mug shots depict Benjamin "Little Bennie" Feldman, 542 W. 112th, Manhattan, owner of the Bango Shipping Company, arrested on the Maryland shore along with two captains, a radioman, and truck drivers. Courtesy of the National Archives.

toms, and the Coast Guard. When trainmen in Baltimore and Wilmington were arrested, they confessed to "spotting" for New York smugglers
for fifty dollars a day.[40]

In the winter or when there was a blockade of New York harbor in
effect, New York smugglers moved liquor operations south to the Gulf
of Mexico. Sim Benoit in Louisiana was paid $350 to transfer liquor
to a fast freight train headed North and to label these cars as "chicken
feed," meaning rice not meant for human consumption. The shipments
were unloaded in Edgewater, New Jersey, and trucked to Manhattan.
When caught, Benoit said he believed that New Jersey police were
part of the racket. This bootlegging enterprise was run by a Newark
gang. In warmer weather, this gang used a tug with three machine guns
mounted on its deck. This tug traveled up and down the East Coast
disbursing liquor.[41]

Temporarily blockading the entrance to New York harbor or stopping smugglers along the Long Island, Connecticut, and New Jersey
coasts never stopped the flow of liquor. Enterprising smugglers simply
landed liquor in New England or the South where it was loaded on to
trucks and trains, supposedly carrying "canned tomatoes" or "chicken
feed," for "bona fide" businesses in New York City.

3

LANDFALL MANHATTAN

Although smugglers had 578 miles of New York City waterfront to choose from, they preferred landing directly at docks on Manhattan's twenty miles of shoreline, in Brooklyn on the East River, across the Hudson in Newark and Hoboken or, if necessary, farther up that river in Yonkers or Kingston. While saving the cost of trucking liquor from Long Island or the Jersey Shore, smuggling directly into the Upper Bay was difficult: it was patrolled by Customs, the Marine Police, and the Coast Guard.

Lower and Upper New York Bays

On clear days, captains of vessels in the Lower Bay could see the city's skyline in the distance. The Woolworth Building dominated the skyline in the early 1920s, the Chrysler Building later in the decade, and the Empire State Building by the final year of Prohibition. Large ships hovered off Ambrose Lightship, marking the beginning of the Ambrose Channel, awaiting pilot boats to guide them through the Narrows to the Upper Bay. Occasionally, rumrunners bypassed Rum Row and came directly to the Lightship to unload liquor onto local speedboats and barges. At night, some turned off all their lights and slipped past patrol boats to reach the Upper Bay.[1]

Once, two miles off Ambrose Lightship, the Coast Guard sighted a Canadian rumrunner alongside an empty sewage barge and several speedboats. The Canadian captain was mortally wounded in the ensuing gunfire and died at Staten Island's Marine Hospital, conscious to the end but unwilling to make a statement. The investigation into his death commended a guardsman for seizing both ship and barge and for seeing that the wounded captain was rushed to the hospital. Investigators also determined the guardsman was not drunk at the time, as the angry Canadian crew maintained, but that he did take a drink immediately after the shooting, coping with the fact that he had probably killed the captain.[2]

Another time, authorities seized a foreign ship, with a reputation for smuggling directly to Manhattan, as it made its way from Ambrose Lightship into the Narrows. This ship belonged to a well-known French bootlegger from St. Pierre and Miquelon rumored to profit $100,000 on each trip to New York City despite the high cost of protection to unload at the docks "without molestation." When this ship was seized, the guardsman in charge shouted at Captain Henri Ducos, "Stick your mitts up, we want to frisk you." The captain replied, "We are very peaceful. I can give you my word of honor about that. These men won't get drunk and will all behave themselves."[3]

Encounters between authorities and smugglers in the Narrows were often dramatic. One night, Customs and Prohibition agents were aboard a Coast Guard boat chasing a rumrunner with thirty-eight longshoremen aboard. It was forced to stop, but then a police boat emerged from the fog and began to shine its searchlight on the Coast Guard for the next twenty minutes, long enough for the longshoremen to toss guns and liquor cases overboard. Later, the commander of the Marine Police Division defended his men observing they were understandably confused. The Coast Guard boat in this case had been the subject of confusion before because it was a former rumrunner converted for Coast Guard use by the agency after it was first seized.[4]

On another occasion in the Narrows, a guardsman with a rifle in his hands jumped from a Coast Guard patrol boat onto a rumrunner while calling loudly for machine-gun backup. He was bluffing and had no backup, but seventeen smugglers surrendered without a fight. After this, the Coast Guard boasted that Rum Row was disappearing due to better enforcement. Mindful of the heroic incident, one news editor drew a quite different conclusion, that Rum Row was disappearing because smugglers were now coming directly into the Upper Bay.[5]

Rumrunners successfully reaching New York harbor mingled among seagoing traffic in the largest port in the United States—ocean liners, merchant ships, mail packets, yachts, fishing trawlers, lumber, coal, and sugar barges, oil tankers, ferries, and speedboats. Usually, smugglers preferred the cover of darkness in the harbor, but at least one rum yacht, bound for the Bronx, successfully hid in broad daylight in the wake of an oil tanker headed for Astoria. One ship, reeking of liquor that could be smelled across the harbor, was detected "zigzagging in a drunken fashion" with fifteen sailors aboard "helplessly intoxicated" and surrounded by five thousand cases of whiskey. The crew was sobered up with coffee and bread after being arrested.[6]

Gunshots could be heard during chases in New York harbor. In one instance, smugglers dodged in and out of traffic while passengers on a ferry watched until the rummies began firing at the Coast Guard. Then the passengers quickly dropped to the deck for protection. Another time the Coast Guard, machine guns blazing and chasing a fast tug in the harbor, deliberately discontinued firing "on account of the proximity of passing ferry boats between Staten Island and New York."[7]

Reputable ocean liners and steamers smuggled liquor. As liners slowed down to dock, passengers and crew passed liquor, purchased abroad, overboard to people in trailing speedboats. Belle Livingstone's elegant night club on Park Avenue obtained its best wines from the captain of a French liner. Musicians, butchers, second cooks, and confectioners on a German liner were caught smuggling liquor to Manhattan. An undercover operation, directed from Washington by Treasury Secretary Andrew Mellon because local Customs officials were suspected of corruption, unmasked a smuggling ring on the Royal Mail Steamer Packet involving a storekeeper, steward, and head-waiter. They were charged with smuggling fifty cases each of Scotch whiskey, French champagne, and morphine. The convicted men received minimal sentences provided "they act as Missionaries to spread the word through the British merchant marine that similar violations will be prosecuted vigorously."[8]

During Prohibition, the Statue of Liberty continued to rule the Upper Bay despite the fact Americans were not at liberty to drink for pleasure. Smugglers coming into the harbor sailed blithely right past the statue. The Coast Guard and Customs anchored large seized ships next to Bedloes Island (now Liberty Island). A photograph of one such ship appeared in the *New York News* with the caption, "Under the Very Eyes of the Bronze Lady." An official Coast Guard photograph documenting the successful seizure of a yacht shows the sleek, low-lying vessel at

Figure 3.1. Liberty and Prohibition

The *Surf*, seized off Montauk, was brought to New York harbor and anchored near the Statue of Liberty. The smugglers on board, dressed in yachting whites, had cruised leisurely back from Rum Row, sure of their cover. But the Coast Guard noticed that the yacht was riding extremely low in the water as if carrying a heavy load. Courtesy of the National Archives.

anchor in front of the Statue of Liberty. Nothing in the photograph suggests that the yachtsmen, cruising in broad daylight toward Manhattan, were smugglers. In fact, they sat on deck in wicker chairs, dressed in yachting whites, leisurely smoking Havana cigars while being served meals and afternoon tea by liveried servants. The yacht even flew the flag of the New York Yacht Club. The smugglers thought they had the perfect cover passing themselves off as wealthy, leisured yachtsmen. But guardsmen, watching through telescopes from a trailing patrol boat, observed that the "yachtsmen's" hands were rough and dirty like those of longshoremen. Most telling, the yacht was riding low in the water as if it carried a heavy load.[9]

Membership in a yacht club did not guarantee immunity from arrest for Prohibition violations. A yacht flying the flag of the New York Yacht Club was inspected four times while anchored at 26th and the East River. Its owner angrily contacted his senator for an explanation. This led to a Coast Guard investigation, which revealed the inspections were triggered by a tip from a crew member's wife upset over a domestic situation. In another case, yacht club member Leland Ross was rescued in a storm after his captain was swept overboard and lost. Ross insisted that the liquor bottles on his yacht were strictly for medicinal use. A yacht anchored at Tebo's Boat Basin in Brooklyn flew the flag of the prestigious New York Athletic Club. The owner, head of a hosiery company in Manhattan, complained after his yacht was searched for liquor, saying he felt that membership in the old, highly respected club "should have been sufficient guarantee of her integrity." M. M. Belding, a New York millionaire silk manufacturer wintering in Miami, was fired on off the Florida coast for failure to stop. Fellow anglers sent telegrams of protest to Secretary of Treasury Mellon while Belding sent one to President Coolidge. The *Miami Herald* editorialized that what had been predicted was coming true: Prohibition was bringing "about a state of affairs more dangerous than the conditions which the amendment (18th) hoped to cure." An unknown but influential New Yorker, whose name was later cut out with scissors from the official record, was angry when his yacht was seized in a Cape Cod harbor after a few bottles of liquor were found aboard during a search. He contacted the district attorney in Boston and his yacht was immediately released.[10]

Stuyvesant Fish, descendant of an old Knickerbocker family, Yale graduate, and member of the Yacht Club and Stock Exchange, ran into trouble with Customs one spring evening while bringing his new yacht into New York harbor accompanied by his wife, teenage sons, and hired captain. A Customs launch approached, ordered the yacht to stop, boarded it, and searched despite Fish's protestations. Afterward, on shore, Fish told reporters no private citizen should be treated this way and pointed out the baby blue curtain on his yacht's windows should have been a dead giveaway that it was not a smuggling operation. Knowing his rights and able to afford a good lawyer, he sued Customs for unlawful search and won: pleasure yachts in the harbor could no longer be searched without prior knowledge that banned cargo was aboard. This was the first case, ten years into Prohibition, in which a Customs or Coast Guard boat was involved in a civil suit for damages because of illegal boarding. Coast Guard Commander F. J. Gorman was concerned because, "Precisely the same routine is gone through with day after day by the Coast Guard in the performance of its general boarding duties," as most U.S. smugglers used vessels documented as "yachts." The U.S. Attorney for the Southern District of New York filed an amended explanation for probable cause for a search of Fish's yacht because letting the ruling stand "would practically stop the Coast Guard and Customs from performing general boarding duties in enforcement of Customs' laws." Fish, having made his point, dropped his suit.[11]

The Hudson River

Smugglers headed up the Hudson River to make deliveries to Manhattan's West Side. If necessary, they went many miles upriver and trucked the liquor back. The owners of Kennedy's Chop House on 121 West 45th Street were suspected of using a yacht owned by James Murphy to smuggle ale through Long Island Sound, up the Harlem River, through Spuyten Duyval Creek, and then eighty miles up the Hudson to a warehouse in Kingston. Then the liquor was trucked back to Manhattan to Fidelity Warehouse at 286 South Street and to another warehouse at 550 Water Street.[12]

This Kennedy family experienced tragedy when the body of twenty-five-year-old Edwin J. Kennedy was found floating in the Hudson off West 84th in 1927. He had been shot in the head. Robbery was not suspected as a motive because a pawn ticket, a diamond ring, and $210 in cash remained in his pockets. Older brother Jack Kennedy, co-owner of the Chop House, insisted that his brother had no enemies and was in excellent spirits before his disappearance. Kennedy's widow told police, "I feel in my heart that he was killed by bootleggers, which one or ones I cannot say." The Coast Guard agreed with her but had no idea who had done it.[13]

One midnight, a Miami sugar freighter dropped liquor and illegal aliens off at the dock near West 36th Street and returned to the Upper Bay. The next morning, the freighter returned to dock with its legitimate load of sugar. It seemed the freighter met up earlier with a Canadian smuggler, one hundred miles off Cape Hatteras, to take on liquor worth half a million dollars. In the process, the Canadian ship was damaged, sank, and the Canadian crew was rescued. Once in New York, long-shoremen unloaded the liquor, the Canadians fled into the city, and the crewmen innocently stayed in their cabins. But the owner of the freighter was arrested anyway because the Coast Guard had picked up indecipherable radio signals from the sinking ship. When the code was finally broken, the case was turned over to Customs because it involved illegal aliens. Coast Guard Intelligence boasted to officials in Washington that this case was "an example of what can be done through the use of intercepted rum-runner's radio traffic."[14]

A curious legal battle over ownership of the Hudson River during Prohibition occurred when a smuggling ship was seized at a dock in Hoboken and charges brought in New Jersey. Although the defense agreed that New York State and New Jersey jointly owned the river bottom, the lawyers cited an obscure antebellum case to prove that New York owned the river itself and the charges should be dropped for lack of jurisdiction. The judge agreed and dismissed the case. The U.S. Department of Justice appealed as the boundaries of the states had been established in the late eighteenth century, each owning half the river. The U.S. Supreme Court eventually ruled to that effect but, in the interim, smugglers chased in New York harbor could head for sanctuary in New Jersey, relying on an obscure law and a friendly judge.[15]

Newark, New Jersey, had a large smuggling syndicate from the earliest days of Prohibition using "British" ships and reputedly making millions in profit. This was the Kinder/Gertner gang, which the Coast Guard discovered owned several "foreign" ships on Rum Row, including some operating off the southern coast. The Coast Guard shot at one of these ships in the Gulf of Mexico, one Canadian sailor died, and the ship sank. Another ship was pirated off the Carolinas and later captured by the Coast Guard, which was surprised to find a crew of pirates as well as smugglers aboard and no one admitting to being captain. Those aboard proved to be "the elite" of the New York/Newark bootlegging world, including Cecil and Charles Kinder. Another of the Kinder/ Gertner ships, which was captured in Yonkers up the Hudson River, yielded up a memorandum book with payoff records for agents, police, and politicians. Fourteen were convicted of smuggling, including the Kinder brothers and the mayor and chief of police of nearby Edgewater, New Jersey.[16]

Neither the Coast Guard nor Customs patrolled the upper Hudson. Little is known about Canadian liquor smuggled south by car or truck to New York City although one enterprising Manhattan taxi owner began smuggling from Montreal, at first using taxis, then trucks, then boats. Authorities also knew that a company based on lower Broadway hired a captain from Hell's Kitchen to take a barge through the New York State Barge Canal to Buffalo. The barge was to bring liquor across the Great Lakes and, perhaps, back through the canal to Albany, and thence down the Hudson.

The last major smuggling effort near New York City involved a wooden World War I cargo ship whose rum captain was given directions by bosses to "Stand up River for Albany." He boldly sailed into the Upper Bay and started up the Hudson River. His ship was identical to a legitimate cargo ship and its name was painted on the stern of the rumrunner. A Staten Island radio unit for the Coast Guard had been monitoring signals from the rum ship while it was in the Lower Bay. When signals suggested the ship was sailing 180 degrees south or north, the Coast Guard assumed it was off the coast of Cape May, New Jersey, and began moving in that direction until the radio signal weakened. This meant the ship was due north, past New York City and heading up the Hudson River! Customs began trailing it. When the rum captain realized that he was being followed, he steered aground at Haverstraw-on-the-Hudson. He and his crew jumped overboard and swam to shore where they were arrested by the local police, Customs, and the Coast Guard.[17]

The East River

The East River was home to many smuggling craft. An anonymous informer, claiming to be connected with the largest rum ring operating in Manhattan, called U.S. District Attorney Emory Buckner to say that a tug with liquor would dock at Pier 31 or 33 on the East River. The tug could be identified by a racehorse painted on its smoke stack. The caller asked Buckner to oversee its capture, although Customs guards were on duty at both piers and the Coast Guard knew the tug was a rumrunner. There was a haze in the lower harbor and a fog in the upper one when the tug entered the Narrows. The Coast Guard chased and fired at it before the patrol boat's engines inexplicably failed. Then the New York Police Marine Division took up the chase, firing at the tug as it fled up the East River. The smugglers deliberately sank the boat at Jefferson Street pier by pulling out the shuttlecocks, and most of the crew escaped. Later, a man named Louis Gertner, 701 West 175th, came to the Barge Office to post bail for the four men captured scuttling the tug. Authorities did not yet know Gertner was affiliated with the Kinder/Gertner gang, and he disappeared when they informed him that whoever posted bail would automatically be given a grand jury subpoena.[18]

Another time a rum yacht, headed down the East River to Gravesend Bay to pick up liquor, caught fire near South Ferry. Captain and crew steered toward Diamond Dredge Barge not knowing it had a ton of dynamite aboard. The Coast Guard raced to rescue the crew on the rum yacht before its three 500 horsepower engines exploded and killed everyone. The rescued men refused to give their names and were not arrested as no liquor was yet aboard.[19]

When Sun Oil Company management suspected its East Coast tankers were illegally picking up liquor on Rum Row, the company hired an undercover detective to confirm this and then alerted authorities. Soon after, a tanker entered New York harbor and was trailed at a discreet distance up the Hudson River by Customs. Then its captain made a U-turn, returned to the harbor, and headed up the East River to Brooklyn to dock at the foot of Court Street. Sixty longshoremen began unloading the liquor. Customs approached in a boat with seventy-five agents aboard ready for a raid. Mistaking the new arrivals for a rival gang, the longshoremen began firing but, after realizing it was the government, the longshoremen tossed their guns into the water so they would not be charged with violating New York's Sullivan gun law. Most gave their legitimate names when arrested; they were primarily German, Jewish, French, and Italian names. A few gave their family name as Doe, including William ("Scottie") Doe, James ("Big Walter") Doe, Raymond ("Sparks") Doe, and Ralph ("Captain Ralph") Doe. Authorities identified the "Does" as bootleg gangsters in Augie Pisano's gang. Pisano handled European liquor landed in Brooklyn destined for Al Capone in Chicago after Frankie Yale's assassination in the mid-1920s. ("Captain Ralph Doe" was probably Capone's older brother visiting New York to oversee such shipments.)[20]

Fulton Fish Market, located on the lower Manhattan side of the East River, near South Street Pier 17 until the operation moved to the Bronx in the early twenty-first century, was popular with smugglers because it was closed at night, its docks and unloading facilities easily accessible. Custom's Deputy Surveyor John McGill, head of the New York harbor patrol, once joked to reporters that he used psychic power to catch smugglers based on information in his dreams, including sending agents to Fulton Market the following morning to search vessels with

Figure 3.2. Rum Fishing Boat Docked at Ellis Island

The fishing boat *Mary of New Bedford*, seen here at Ellis island, was stopped and searched several times in Long Island Sound. Courtesy of the National Archives.

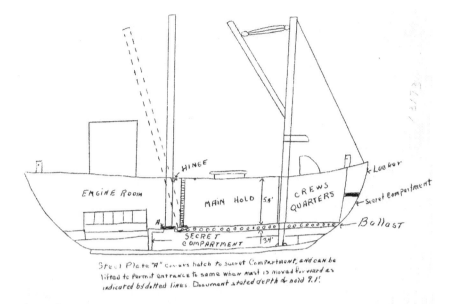

Figure 3.3. Hidden Compartment for Liquor
This Coast Guard drawing of *Mary of New Bedford* shows a hidden compartment for liquor. Courtesy of the National Archives.

names similar to those in his dreams. Once he dreamed of a fishing boat named the *South Carolina,* and his agents searched but could only find one named the *Caroline.* He said that was close enough, and a search under the fish revealed liquor cases. A Coast Guard Commander in New York City complained, perhaps after reading about McGill's technique in the newspapers, that Customs was not seriously scrutinizing the Market. McGill's staff was soon tripled because serious searches at the Market required more than psychic powers and six-foot probes to test for liquor cases buried under tons of fish. Success required agents to take time-consuming, detailed, interior measurements of fishing boats and compare these to fishing licenses to detect hidden compartments and false bottoms.[21]

A reputable fishing import company's appraiser, while checking five hundred barrels of herring at Brooklyn Yard, found expensive, old whiskey at the bottom of the first barrel. He checked the entire shipment and found smuggled whiskey in every barrel and reported this to the authorities. Fish dealers in Halifax, Nova Scotia, insisted they were not responsible as they shipped mackerel, not herring, on that ship. They suspected a wealthy Halifax newcomer, with a new car and house, as the shipper of the herring. Canadian editors observed this seizure was "a reminder, if one were necessary that bootlegging has been a 'minor industry' in Newfoundland, as in many countries. That, of itself, is sufficiently unpleasant. Whatever the opinions the people of the United States may have as to the Eighteenth Amendment, wets and drys, with rare exception, very properly resent assistance given by alien countries in violation of the United States Constitution or laws."[22]

A boat, long suspected of piracy on Rum Row, docked at 155th and the Harlem River under the watchful eye of a Customs guard. When he left to make a phone call, possibly to ask for reinforcements, he returned to find ten men swarming about the boat's deck and five cars parked nearby for loading. He challenged them, but they insisted they were policemen, showed their badges, and peppered him with questions. When he refused to answer, they left.[23]

Although the Bronx shoreline is minimal, a smuggling fleet estimated at one hundred craft was located in a marina at 132nd Street and Locust Avenue. This was a desirable location: contact boats could either travel down the East River, through the harbor and out to sea or venture through the turbulent waters of Hell Gate to Long Island Sound and past Montauk to Rum Row.[24]

Landfall: The Battery

Captured smugglers were booked at the Custom's Barge Office adjacent to the ferry terminals at the southernmost tip of Manhattan. Sailors were often drunk when they were arrested: they knew they could not be interrogated unless they were sober. This gave their employers time to send lawyers to the Barge Office to have them quickly released on bail. Once, a drunk crew pelted reporters and photographers with hard-boiled eggs and potatoes. Another time, a drunk crew yelled to reporters that they could sell them a case of scotch for five cents.

Lawyers posting bail at the Barge Office affirmed that rum captains and rum sailors were their clients even though the lawyers had never met them. This was the first indication for Coast Guard and Customs officials that they were dealing with well-organized and well-funded smuggling syndicates. Once, rum sailors were arrested and, in anticipa-

Figure 3.4. Booking at the Barge Office
This captured rum crew was booked at the Barge Office on the southern tip of Manhattan. Courtesy of the National Archives.

tion of bail being posted, dressed themselves for a night on the town and were deeply disappointed when they learned it was too late for bail. Told they would appear before a grand jury in the morning, they drowned their sorrows in liquor still stored on their ship. Several were wanted men who entered the courtroom the following morning with bravado singing sea shanties.[25]

In Manhattan, public auctions of seized vessels were held in Dead Man's Basin next to the Barge Office at Battery Point. Often boats auctioned off were sold back to the same gangs, which used dummy purchasers as intermediaries. Profits from smuggling were more than enough to cover repurchase several times over. In one case, a ship was seized four times in one year, bought back just as many times and, in the interval, made many profitable trips. There were good deals at these auctions: a forty-foot cabin cruiser, which cost $30,000 to build, sold for a mere $1,000. On the other hand, the Coast Guard had first rights to seized vessels and acquired several hundred in this way. This could lead to mix-ups later at sea. Such Coast Guard boats were sometimes mistaken by the Marine Police or Customs for smugglers.[26]

While rum captains lived throughout the city, many lived in Lower Manhattan near the Battery and Fulton Fish Market. Captain Browne-Willis, known as "Whiskers" because of his "Prince Albert Beard," lodged at #2 Fulton Street. Caught smuggling into New York harbor on his thirteenth trip, he and his sailors insisted the liquor aboard was never intended for Manhattan. Browne-Willis seemed to lead a charmed life. Once, when a rival gang took a shot at him in a Bronx Park, a metal eyeglass container in the pocket over his heart deflected the bullet into his arm, and he survived. Indicted eleven times for rumrunning, this was his first time in court in Manhattan. He dressed to impress the jury but was judged guilty along with Max Bernstein and Harry Gordon, owners of the liquor cargo. They served their sentences, but Browne-Willis jumped bail and disappeared.[27]

Captain George Jeffries, hoping to mitigate his sentence when he was caught in New York harbor on his fortieth trip, willingly gave the names of the gangsters for whom he smuggled. He mentioned the names of Bill Dwyer, Waxey Gordon, Manny Wexler, Frank Costello, George Ziebling, Phil Coffey, and Sig Rosenbloom. The captain also offered to show the different sites where he dropped the liquor, but authorities did not follow up fearing that to do so would imperil his life. According to the captain, all monetary transactions were done from a midtown office on Broadway. No cash was used on Rum Row. This was to discourage robberies by "go through" pirates who stole cash rather than liquor. Usually transfers of liquor were authorized by matching a torn playing card or a torn dollar bill, the supercargo having one portion and the captain from shore having the other. Captain Jeffries had neither torn card nor bill. He used a special ticket obtained before leaving shore at a Broadway office. When questioned by authorities, he could not recall the office's location. A subsequent search of his luggage produced a calling card belonging to Nookie Collins, "The Big Lobster Merchant," specializing in "Skotch Tweed." On the reverse the captain had written in pencil—#1261 Broadway, Room 502, with the notation "Get off [at] 34th Street."[28]

Several hundred New Yorkers captained rum ships and speedboats besides McCoy, Browne-Willis, and Jeffries. There is little information on them unless they were captured. After the laws were tightened at the end of Prohibition making jail terms likely, most captains disappeared

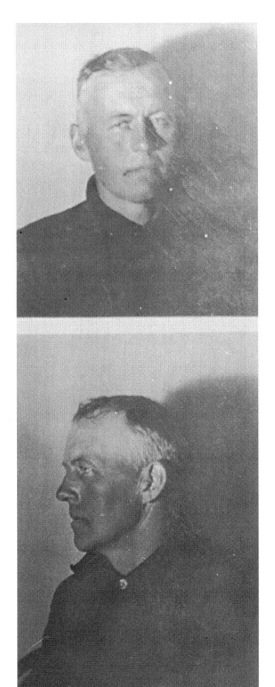

Figure 3.5. Rum Captain
Mug shots of Captain Axel
Ohlsen, 2646 Mansfield
Place, Brooklyn, were taken
after he was arrested for
smuggling to New York via
Chesapeake Bay. Courtesy of
the National Archives.

after their boat was seized and before it reached the Barge Office. Available information suggests that the captains ran the gamut from tough to polite and respectful, from talkative to silent.

Captain Arthur G. Stone (alias George H. Miles) was a sinister character who collected his crew around Murphy's Saloon and among drug dealers. A Lieutenant Commander in the United States Navy in World War I, he had been jailed in the early 1920s for killing a sailor on a commercial ship he commanded. The Coast Guard met him "innocently" when it boarded his yacht in Gravesend Bay and again off the coast of South Carolina. There he was arrested after bragging in a bar in Norfolk that he planned to smuggle aliens and liquor from Cuba.[29]

Captain William Rhoades, seized smuggling in a yacht off Port Jefferson, Long Island Sound, surprised captors as he was "a college graduate, a fraternity man, the son of a preacher, and quite different from any other rum captain." Eventually, he turned government witness and ceased smuggling. Captain Charles Newton of New York City, seized on a rumrunner in Delaware Bay, was unshaven and roughly dressed but impressed captors as "a man of education and greater ability than his appearance indicated." Newton admitted that he was smuggling, said he did not care what charges were presented against him, and would not give information on anyone else.[30]

Captain Snow, captured aboard a rumrunner in the Hudson River, was known to Coast Guard intelligence as a bigamist with wives in New York, Boston, and Halifax: they knew about each other but didn't mind as he supported each in style. Captain Charles Samuel Forde was once an enlisted Coast Guardsman before hiring on as captain of an oil tanker, which smuggled liquor. Captain Alexander Tanos, in a vessel owned by the Atlantic Coast Towing and Transportation Company of New York City, insisted he hadn't known the tug had a double-bottom capable of holding three thousand cases of liquor. African-American Captain Anthony Crawford managed a crew consisting of white European immigrants. Captain Roscoe Jenkins, a former Manhattan policeman, and his crew were lost in a storm at sea. Captain William P. Cluett, mortally wounded by the Coast Guard off Lightship Ambrose, left a pregnant wife and children in Canada. His pastor in the funeral eulogy described him as "a fine churchman, thorough going and well instructed, a good husband and father, a good friend, and a master mariner."[31]

Hundreds, probably thousands, of rum sailors lived in New York City, most of them in lower Manhattan and Brooklyn. Many lodged at the Seaman's Church Institute, 25 South Street, which began as a floating chapel off the Battery in the nineteenth century. Sailors, who could not be induced to sign up as smugglers with good pay and easy access to liquor, were sometimes tricked into service. On Rum Row, the Coast Guard once rescued four sailors who had been shanghaied. They stood on the deck of a rumrunner and held up a blanket as a signal of distress. A cook, who signed to work on a barge headed for the Caribbean, discovered at sea the barge was going to Nova Scotia to pick up liquor to resell along the U.S. coast before heading for Nassau. When the ship finally arrived in Nassau, he went to the U.S. consulate to lodge a complaint saying he had been intimidated into staying aboard by the captain's arsenal of ten pistols and eight rifles.[32]

Many rum sailors were Scandinavian-Americans. The crew of a mackerel schooner seized on the East Rivet included: Harry Anderson, 72 South Street, Harry Thorsen, John Olsen, Pete Anderson, and Charles Ioarsen from the Seaman's Institute, and Karl Carlsen, Leif Hanson, and Burger Nichelsen from Brooklyn. When a steamship was seized off the Rockaways running without lights on a moonlit night, sailors Erickson and Olson were arrested. Sailors on a rum speedboat seized off Sandy Hook were a more mixed lot: Joseph Wilson, and John Dykes, 25 South Street, Henry Wolf and Hans Karlsen from Brooklyn, B. L. Smith from the Bronx. J. J. Malloy was noted in arrest records as "a Jew in spite of his name."[33]

A detailed inventory of a crew's locker contents, aboard one seized rum tug, gives an interesting perspective on what the men took to sea. Three deck hands, recruited from the Seaman's Institute, had between them—one rubber suit, one leather vest, neckties, suit, flashlight, a pair of rubber boots, overshoes, two other pairs of shoes, two shirts, one handbag, one pair shoes, one flashlight, two dozen soaps, one pair binoculars, one watch and chain, a kilogram of tea, and $99 in cash. The cook, also recruited from the Institute, had a watch, a box, one pair of shorts, three pairs of boots, one sweater, two knives, and an egg beater. A fireman living at 2 Front Street, Manhattan, owned one pair of shoes, one pair of overalls, one shirt, and one pair of pants. Another fireman, recruited from the Institute, had no personal property nor did one deck hand. The oiler, from Brooklyn, had two jumpsuits, one pair of overalls, one flashlight, one pair of gloves, one towel, and $20. Another fireman, also from Brooklyn, had a handbag, pair of woolen hose, two jumpers, two suits, underwear, one shaving outfit, one pair of shoes, and one sweater. The electrician, from New Jersey, had a tool chest, handbag, leather parcel, watch, two complete overall suits, three shirts, one white shirt, one pair of shoes, one pair of rubbers, one clock, two flashlights, and $9. Captain Charles Sawyer, 370 East 23rd Street, Manhattan, had a handbag, pair of shoes, pair of leather boots, one cap, pair of rubbers, pair of gloves, pair of khaki pants, barometer, and $100.[34]

Supercargoes on rum ships supervised the liquor cargo. Most were from New York City. Joe Romero, alias Avalino Escuria Lopez, was arrested aboard a rum ship headed for East 70th Street. He had three thousand dollars and a diamond ring. Charles Levy, 245 West 51st Street, was supercargo on a coal ship carrying liquor up the Hudson River. He was arrested by authorities in Havana, at the request of the Coast Guard, while he was awaiting the arrival of another ship. He was described in the records as a well-dressed New York Jew with a fondness for "obscene poetry." In a letter to his sister in New York City, seized and opened before it could be mailed, he had written, "Felix and the boys had a dinner the other night for some pal of theirs that is going back to Spain. Was a tame affair as no one got arrested." James Regno, Levy's New York partner, was also arrested in Havana and his letters likewise seized. Regno wrote a lady friend, "I haven't much to say because everything looks bad. . . . They have either double-crossed us or done something wrong . . . I am losing money and nothing to show [for it] but there is no use to worry if I come back I will get my boat and come right back here, for there is plenty of work here."[35]

Three supercargoes, aboard a Miami sugar freighter bound for Manhattan and suspected of being on board to supervise liquor to be picked up off Rum Row, were described by Customs as: a man with a "Jewish nose;" a Canadian who was "good looking of the French type"; and an "ordinary-looking American." James Pond, supercargo on a Brooklyn fishing schooner, did not admit he was supervising a hidden liquor cargo under the fish, and gave his occupation as assistant circulation manager of the "New York Press," 145 West 45th, which the Coast Guard later learned was actually the address of a horse tipping office. Max Schaefer, a well-dressed supercargo, "did not have the outward appearance of a working man." Two supercargoes, George Ferguson and Charles Smith, worked for New York syndicate boss Bill Dwyer: Ferguson accompanied a shipment from Canada to a Manhattan dock and Smith later perjured himself as a witness against Dwyer. Most supercargoes escaped arrest because they carried cash to bribe their way free: Captain Jeffries' supercargo escaped with $600 cash kept for that express purpose, and Jeffries said, "If the Coast Guard did not want him to escape, he could not have done so."[36]

In Their Own Words

The Coast Guard recognized one rumrunner despite a crew member placing a fake name on a piece of tin over its stern before it entered the Upper Bay. After the ship was seized, captain, first mate, cook, and supercargo were closely questioned. The interrogator asked why the name was changed at sea and was told that they thought they might get held up by hijackers. The captain reported that his mate said the safest way was to change the name. The interrogator observed hijackers care little about a vessel's name and then read aloud a letter, found in the captain's trunk, because the captain claimed he could not read. The letter, written by one of the captain's children, began, "My dear father . . . We herd [sic] here where you is going to and you must be careful and not get caught. Seven years in prison if you get caught."

The interrogator told the captain, "We know that this business is conducted by somebody who furnishes the funds and that they hire you fellows [captains] to do it. I will frankly tell you we would like to get the fellows higher up instead of the poor devils who are hired to do it. Of course, you can make your choice." The captain said, "That is all I know about it."

The cook, asked why the ship's name was changed, replied, "A cook in the galley don't know anything about those things." The first mate also said he didn't know who had changed the name. Asked if he helped, he said, "Yes." Asked if he did it under orders, he said, "Sure." Asked who gave the orders, he exclaimed, "My God! Now you have me. . . . Who I am working for? I don't know."

The passenger suspected of being the supercargo insisted he was a cousin to the captain's wife and merely came along for the trip. When asked by his interrogator to give this cousin's name, the supercargo made one up and was caught in a lie because the interrogator had interviewed the captain first and knew the wife's name. The supercargo exclaimed, "I am in trouble. I see that. I realize that." His interrogator said, "You started with a story, that you cannot maintain, a story that is not true. You are no more related to the captain than I am. . . . And you are no cousin to his wife!" To which the other replied, "You are asking me too much, Sir!"[37]

Captains, sailors, cooks, and supercargoes on rumrunners that successfully delivered liquor were paid off and avoided interrogations and arrests. If caught, they knew they would be quickly released on bond and could go to sea once more. Owners could also post bond and continue to use their vessels until a final judgment which could take months or years. These owners also knew that if they had to forfeit a rumrunner, there was a good chance they could buy it back again at public auction.

One Coast Guard officer in New York City found the entire process discouraging. The rum ship, whose captain, cook, first mate, and supercargo had been interrogated at length over use of a fake name, had to be released on bond while the case was pending in court. Meanwhile the rumrunner returned to Canada for another load and soon hovered again outside the Narrows in the Lower Bay. "What is $7,500 [price of the bond] to that ring," the Coast Guard officer queried his superiors. "I look upon the release [of the ship under bond] as a betrayal of the forces of the Federal government. . . . I imagine our people feel that they have been jousting at windmills."[38]

4

THE BROADWAY MOB

Most Americans are taught that Prohibition spurred the development of the U.S. Underworld, but few know exactly how this happened. New York City's large, liquor-smuggling syndicates emerged from well-known neighborhood gangs in Manhattan on the Lower East Side, the West Side, and Little Italy. These new syndicates diverted legally-produced, domestic liquor intended for industrial, military, medicinal, and religious uses. They marketed this diverted liquor, along with smuggled liquor, to thousands of bootleggers supplying night clubs, speakeasies, drugstores, and individuals.

Lower East Side

The Lower East Side, bounded by the East River, the infamous Bowery, and 14th Street, was once home to the legendary McGurk's Suicide Hall, a saloon famous for knife fights, flying glasses of ale, and a high mortality rate for those brave enough to enter and order a drink. The neighborhood housed immigrants from Southern and Eastern Europe crammed into six-story tenements on twenty-five-foot by one-hundred-foot lots, with little natural light, twenty-four families to a building. Reformers claimed Prohibition would clean up the Bowery, but it remained wide-open for drinking: secretive passwords and cards, used at night clubs and speakeasies elsewhere in the city, were not needed on the Bowery.[1]

There were five hundred synagogues in Lower East Side neighborhoods to accommodate the flood of immigrants. Jewish religious wine stores in the neighborhood remained open. The Volstead Act permitted a Jewish family to have from two to ten gallons a year for home services. (Catholic and Protestant churches also had continued access to wine for communion services.) Circumventing of Prohibition began with these wine stores dispensing far more than needed for religious purposes. The Prohibition Bureau hired Isadore "Izzy" Einstein, an immigrant Austrian-Jewish postal worker from the neighborhood who understood German, Hungarian, Yiddish, Polish, French, Italian, Russian, and a little Chinese, to investigate legal shipments to religious wine stores. He discovered that two hundred people were bootlegging, including rabbis knowingly reselling wine permits, a fake rabbi serving seventy congregations, a genuine rabbi claiming a congregation ten times its actual size, and rabbis with very Irish names like Sullivan and Moriarty. Einstein also discovered "synagogues" located in apartments, butcher shops, pool parlors, and one pork store. Wine stores were then closed and wine distributed only within legitimate synagogues.[2]

Monk Eastman, commanding fifteen hundred men in the Lower East Side's largest pre-Prohibition gang, might have been expected to dominate smuggling and bootlegging in his neighborhood, but he was murdered in 1920. He was shot in front of a café in Union Square in an altercation with a drunken "friend," an employee, ironically, of the new Prohibition agency. Instead, Arnold Rothstein, thirty-eight, black sheep of a wealthy German-Jewish family from the upper West Side and a longtime associate of Eastman, became the kingpin of smuggling and bootlegging in Manhattan. As a teenager, Rothstein worked as a translator for immigrants dealing with Tammany bosses before he ventured into gambling. A successful underworld figure by 1920, he was able to provide loans to fellow gangsters. He had a reputation for gambling on a sure thing, and smuggling liquor seemed to fit that requirement. With advance knowledge of the rigged 1919 World Series, known as the Black Sox Scandal, he may have used winnings from that for start-up funds for smugglers and bootleggers.[3]

Rothstein's first foray into liquor smuggling was with "Waxey" Gordon (also known as Irving Wexler), former pickpocket and labor "thug" on the Lower East Side. They met on a bench in Central Park to discuss a partnership and began smuggling to eastern Long Island by

Figure 4.1. Manhattan's Underworld King

Arnold Rothstein was a New York gambler who financed the purchase of liquor abroad for several gangs. He was murdered over a gambling debt in the fall of 1928. Courtesy of the Library of Congress.

bribing a local Coast Guard commander. They had a fleet of trucks to move the liquor to warehouses in Queens. When the commander was replaced, their next shipment had to be diverted at the last minute to the West Indies and sold at cost. This was too close a call for Rothstein who retreated into the background, leaving the field to Gordon while remaining a major financial backer. Gordon's operation flourished for the next few years.

A lumber barge, used to smuggle liquor for Gordon, was seized near New York in 1925. Captain Hans Fuhrman agreed to testify against his boss. Supposedly, Mrs. Fuhrman had asked Gordon not to employ her husband as he was alcoholic and returned home from sea drunk and penniless. Her request was refused, and she may have tipped authorities about her husband's last voyage. Federal authorities also raided Gordon's headquarters in the midtown Knickerbocker Building, obtaining incriminating documents including maps and names of contacts. Fuhrman, kept in a guarded Manhattan hotel room, died before any trial could take place. Police ruled his death a suicide, but his wife insisted he was murdered. The U.S. District Attorney for Southern New York incredulously told a Congressional committee investigating Prohibition enforcement, "There was the most important witness in our first direct challenge to a big, wealthy, powerful and hitherto unmolested gang of bootleggers, and our most important witness committed suicide within three weeks." Four witnesses against Gordon were murdered before his next encounter with the law, suggesting that Mrs. Fuhrman was right.[4]

After this close call, Gordon followed in Rothstein's steps and quit smuggling realizing he could be convicted on the word of any one of the many captains working for him. He took his millions and invested in illegal breweries in Elizabeth, Union City, Patterson, and Newark, New Jersey, illegal distilleries in Pennsylvania and New York, and Manhattan night clubs. His wealth increased: he traveled abroad with his family and bought a "castle" with a moat on the Jersey Shore.

Jacob "Little Augie" Orgen was also a product of the Lower East Side. He was murdered in a drive-by shooting in 1927 by his own "muscle men," Jacob "Gurrah" Shapiro and Louis "Lepke" Buchalter. Jack "Legs" Diamond (John T. Nolan), Orgen's bodyguard, took over his bootleg operations, Shapiro took over labor racketeering, and Buchalter controlled the murder business, eventually heading a 1930s murder-for-hire operation known as Murder Incorporated.[5]

Maier Suchowljansky, eighteen, and Benjamin "Bugsy" Siegel, fifteen, had the "Bugs and Meyer" gang on the Lower East Side before Prohibition. When he was nine, Suchowljansky's family emigrated from Poland to the Lower East Side. Siegel grew up "over the Bridge" in Brooklyn. At the start of Prohibition, the two teenagers worked as enforcers for other bootleggers, hijacking liquor convoys or, conversely, riding shotgun to protect the convoys. Siegel, in particular, gained a reputation as a killer-for-hire, supposedly going "Bugsy" in the process of murdering someone.[6]

Arthur Flegenheimer, another Jewish teenager in 1920, began as a lone gangster, not on the Lower East Side but in the Bronx. He rose to the top in a bootleg street gang and emerged on the public scene in the late 1920s as the infamous Dutch Schultz, engaged in a bootleg war for control of the city's beer supply. He also took over the Harlem numbers racket, founded by independent black businessmen.[7]

Hell's Kitchen on the West Side

Hell's Kitchen, stretching from 23rd Street to the fifties in the area west of Ninth Avenue to the Hudson River, encompassed slaughter houses, docks, freight yards, and tenements inhabited by a large number of Irish immigrants. The railroad yards were frequently targets for robbery by two large pre-Prohibition neighborhood gangs, the Hudson Dusters and the Gophers. A smuggling syndicate, rivaling Gordon's on the Lower East Side, emerged in Hell's Kitchen under William "Big Bill" Dwyer. Born and raised in the neighborhood, the Irish-American Dwyer had ushered in vaudeville houses in his youth. At the start of Prohibition, he worked as a stevedore in the Longshoreman's Union. With his union contacts, including truckers, garages, docks, and warehouses, Dwyer quickly developed his smuggling syndicate. Like Gordon on the East Side, he initially relied on Arnold Rothstein for funding.[8]

Dwyer's syndicate was expert at bribing politicians, police, and federal agents. Top associates were "Broadway Bill" Duffy, John McCambridge, Walter Weider, and Max Bernstein. The syndicate maintained a fleet of contact boats near the East River's Hell Gate Bridge and operational headquarters in Times Square. Verbal deals, in the hundreds of thousands of dollars, were witnessed by lawyers each week. When "Legs"

Diamond began hijacking Dwyer's truck convoys, Dwyer cut ties with Rothstein believing the latter was backing Diamond. This was probably when Dwyer turned to piracy on Rum Row to obtain liquor, looting at least one ship and removing $800,000 worth of liquor.[9]

Authorities developed leads about Dwyer's smuggling syndicate, about the same time they were closing in on Waxey Gordon. An armed speedboat, used to decoy the Coast Guard on Rum Row, was captured and a William Duffy, who had a tavern on Broadway, a "wide-open bar-room," proved to own the speedboat. Duffy also owned the Sea Grille on West 45th and managed the Silver Slipper night club. Authorities suspected that the gang met on the second floor of Dinty Moore's Restaurant at 216 West 46th, "late at night drinking bottled Canadian ale." The Coast Guard learned, from an aggrieved family member of a sailor on a Dwyer boat lost at sea, that John McCambridge had an office on Pier 38 on the Hudson River. There "negro crews" of long-shoremen bossed by "Big Riley" unloaded liquor cases into furniture vans for distribution.[10]

Then an undercover Customs guard, in a Manhattan speakeasy, overheard that a coal steamer smuggling liquor was expected in the Hudson, despite a Coast Guard blockade of the harbor. The steamer was seized off the dock at Dyckman Street. Its owners were McCambridge and A. M. Eversole. The Washington Post reported that this was "the first known case" in which a large ship had "successfully eluded the rum chasers and slipped into the harbor . . . the most daring in the history of Customs and Prohibition laws." Not one of the officers on board had a license, there was no list of crew members, and no ship's log.[11]

Even though it was a hot day in the summer, Captain Snow and a crew of twenty-five were wearing kid gloves to unload liquor. Yet a search uncovered only eighteen bottles on board. Snow's tally book showed that the liquor had already been unloaded to another boat on the river, but Customs had watched the ship closely the preceding two weeks and had seen no such transfer. The Coast Guard towed the steamer south to Bedloes Island with one smuggler at the wheel. He tried to steer it aground at 17th Street in Hoboken, but his maneuver was averted at the last minute. This raised suspicions that there might be more liquor aboard, and a second search revealed three thousand cases of liquor underneath hundreds of tons of coal.

The big break against the Dwyer syndicate came from a Canadian engineer on another coal ship, befriended by a supercargo named George

Ferguson. The supercargo bragged that he had been hired by Dwyer at a Montreal race track, that Dwyer smuggled more liquor into New York City than anyone else, and that this trip would be one of Dwyer's biggest hauls. The engineer also said that a Coast Guard patrol boat met the ship at sea and escorted it into the harbor at night, with its searchlight on, all the way into the dock at East Fourth where the liquor was unloaded onto a large truck painted with signs for a newspaper company. Before daybreak, empty of liquor but still smelling of it, the coal boat moved to the Grand Street wharf. In the morning, it was boarded by an officer from the corrupt patrol boat as if he planned to search it. He went directly into the wheelhouse for a private meeting with the captain and mate because he knew there was no liquor aboard.[12]

In the same way that Captain Fuhrman was a weak link in the Gordon syndicate, so Supercargo Ferguson was the weak link in Dwyer's. U.S. District Attorney Emory Buckner, forced earlier by Fuhrman's death to drop the conspiracy case against Gordon, now charged the Dwyer syndicate with conspiracy, naming more than fifty New Yorkers as defendants to be tried in two separate trials beginning the summer of 1926 in the federal courthouse in Manhattan. That same summer, the Coast Guard seized a rumrunner off the Carolinas with "a surprisingly large number of the elite of the bootleg world . . . big operators in the vicinity of New York," including Weider, Duffy, Cliff, and Cecil Kinder, from a Newark/Chicago syndicate, and Max Phaff arrested in Paris two years before in the piracy of a French ship.[13]

Evidence offered in the first trial included the Dwyer syndicate's use of corrupted Coast Guard patrol boats and its bribing of federal agents with Broadway dinners, theater tickets, prostitutes, and hotel suites. Coast Guard authorities already had some idea that the agency had been corrupted. In one case, two crew members on a German ship jumped overboard seeking asylum and were rescued by the Coast Guard: they told the officer questioning them that their ship unloaded liquor off Fire Island to Coast Guard patrol boats #103 and #106. The officer thought that they said this to get him to take them into New York City, where their chances of asylum would be better, and returned them to their ship but suggested in his report that those two patrol boats should be closely watched. In another case, two Prohibition agents watching the harbor reported seeing liquor transferred from a captured rum ship to a trailing patrol boat named the *Calumet*. According to Coast Guard Intelligence Officer Charles Root, the agency believed guardsmen on patrol boats operating close to shore were susceptible to corruption because they were not as well-trained or as well-paid as career men serving on destroyers and cruisers at sea. The fact that the Dwyer syndicate deliberately painted one of its boats to look like a patrol boat, escorting ships into the harbor, might have also distorted reports of corruption. Coast Guard historian Malcolm Willoughby later defended the agency noting that guardsmen were as divided personally on Prohibition as the general population and dealt on a daily basis with temptations and bribes. Yet corrupted guardsmen comprised a small proportion of the Coast Guard during Prohibition.[14]

Dwyer and his payoff agent were convicted, but everyone else in the first trial was judged not guilty. After a year in prison, Dwyer quit

Figure 4.2. Temptation
Coast Guardsmen are here overseeing a typical confiscation of liquor. The bottles were wrapped in packages so glass would not break during the transferral on Rum Row. The Coast Guard, Prohibition Bureau, Customs, and police were liable to corruption by smugglers and bootleggers. Courtesy of the National Archives.

smuggling to become a silent partner in the Phoenix Cereal Company, the former Clausen and Flanigan Brewery at West 26th and 10th. The Phoenix was to become the largest illegal brewery in Manhattan. Legitimate breweries in the city had either switched to producing soft drinks or ice cream after 1920 or were licensed to produce "near" beer. Federal agents unsuccessfully sought four times to obtain a warrant to raid the West Side brewery. They were successful in the final year of Prohibition when they found a judge willing to say that smelling beer from the nearby street was sufficient for a warrant.

Dwyer's public partner in the brewery was Owney Madden, released from Sing Sing in 1923 after serving time for murder. Dwyer took him aboard after Madden began hijacking his liquor trucks. The top-selling beer of the brewery became "Madden's No. 1." Dwyer, Madden, and Frenchy de Magne, a third partner, bought political protection for the brewery from West Side politician James J. Hines who conveniently owned a trucking company probably used to distribute the beer. Then, the beer was sold to Tammany politicians who marked it up 50 percent for resale to speakeasies and clubs in their wards and precincts. Madden soon had money to invest in night clubs, including the Cotton Club, Silver Slipper, and Park Avenue Club, while also having interests in boxing and laundry rackets.[15]

Major Irish-American bootleg gangsters in New York City, besides Dwyer, Duffy, and Madden, were Larry Fay and Charles "Vinnie" Higgins. Fay, a member of the West Side's old Hudson Duster gang, moved into the taxi business with money from a win at the races or from Rothstein. By 1920, Fay controlled taxi stands in front of Grand Central and Penn Station and worked with Hines in a protection racket involving small milk producers. Fay began smuggling liquor from Montreal in taxis, then in trucks, and finally in fishing schooners. Eventually, he took his money and invested in night clubs, including several named after himself such as El Fay and Fay's Follies. Higgins operated in both Manhattan and Brooklyn, the latter putting him in competition with the Italian syndicate of Frankie Yale. Once, Higgins piloted a plane to Sing Sing to have lunch with the warden, a childhood friend. When Governor Roosevelt learned of this, he disciplined the warden. Higgins survived being shot twice, knifed once, and questioned eight times in homicide investigations. One summer evening in the early 1930s, he was murdered in Brooklyn emerging from his young daughter's dance recital, but not before he ran down an alley to draw the bullets away from his family.[16]

The city's most powerful Irish-American bootleg gangster was not the least bit Irish: he was 100 percent Italian. Frank Costello, born Francesco Castiglia on the Italian mainland, emigrated as a young child with his family to East Harlem's Little Italy. He changed his name to Costello, the Irish-sounding equivalent of Castiglia, before Prohibition when he realized that the Irish controlled the police and dominated the corrupt Tammany political machine. He moved so much within Irish and Jewish social circles (his wife was German-Jewish) that authorities never suspected he was Italian or had connections with Italian gangsters. He was misidentified as an unimportant underling in the Dwyer syndicate and charged in the second trial in 1927. Unlike the flashy Dwyer, Costello deliberately maintained a low profile and benefited from a hung jury. Later he privately claimed he bribed a juror. He was never retried because his records were conveniently "lost." The federal judge in this trial resigned a few years later amid charges of corruption.[17]

Costello took over the Dwyer operation when the latter was imprisoned. Costello's headquarters were near or in the new Chrysler Building. His syndicate owned European freighters such as the *Napoli, Sicilia, Bel Vino, Nonte,* and *Pollino* with foreigners fronting as owners, warehouses in St. Pierre and Miquelon in the North Atlantic, and a domestic fleet of small boats on the East River. While he was known to the public as a flourishing bootlegger, few knew he was a major figure in the Underworld. Supposedly, John J. Raskob, manager of Governor Smith's presidential campaign, invited Costello to bring a fellow bootlegger to meet the candidate. Smith advised the two "bootleggers" to prepare for an end to Prohibition because he expected to win as a Wet.[18]

Little Italy

A major Italian-American syndicate emerged in Manhattan's Little Italy. Before Prohibition, the *Unione Sicilione* was confined to Italian neighborhoods in Manhattan and Brooklyn. The *Unione* concentrated on traditional crimes such as gambling, prostitution, and protection rackets. Its headquarters were in an Italian restaurant and Marinelli's Garage, both at the intersection of Kenmare and Mulberry. Albert Marinelli, owner of a trucking business, was also a Tammany politician with two hundred thugs on call for use on election days. Here Sicilian-born Chief Joe Masseria met with top "soldiers," including Salvatore Lucania and

Joseph Doto. Lucania, twenty-three, who was born in Palermo, arrived in New York City at the age of nine and grew up on the Lower East Side. He was in the pre-Prohibition Five Points Gang and, in 1922, killed Rocco Valenti, a rival to Masseria, on orders from his boss. Doto, eighteen, was born in Montemarano.[19]

New York Police Department headquarters were at 240 Centre between Grand and Broome streets on the edge of Little Italy. The NYPD could have kept a close eye on these neighboring Italians during Prohibition—except its Italian-speaking detective squad was inexplicably disbanded in 1920. "Bootleggers' Row," a curbside black market in liquor serving the entire city, emerged that same year on Kenmare, Broome, Grand, and Elizabeth streets, ostensibly under the protection of Masseria. Gangsters from throughout the city bought and sold fake and genuine permits to forty million gallons of pre-Prohibition liquor stored in government warehouses. They also robbed private bonded liquor warehouses, like Republic Storage at West 34th Street. In addition, fifty thousand Italian-American homes in tenements throughout the city began producing wine and gin for the black market. Gutters in Little Italy and Greenwich Village ran purple each fall from winemaking.[20]

The *Unione Sicilione* might have become rich bootlegging and smuggling if Masseria had chosen to operate beyond Italian neighborhoods. But he was an old-time boss, known as a "moustache Pete," and did not recognize or act on the opportunity. If Al Capone and Johnny Torrio had not moved from New York to Chicago prior to Prohibition, New York City's Prohibition history might have been very different, probably more violent. On a visit to Manhattan early in Prohibition, Capone dined with friends in Little Italy, including Lucania and Doto, and challenged them to seize the day as he and Torrio were doing in Chicago.

Lucania and Doto listened and began their own smuggling ring with Masseria's blessing, as long as they remained loyal. This ring included Albert Anastasia, Vito Genovese, and Thomas Lucchese as enforcers. Costello was invited and brought his smuggling experience with Dwyer's West Side gang. Suchowljansky was included because he and Lucania were friends. (They met on the Lower East Side as teenagers: Lucania admired him for fighting back when Lucania tried to steal his lunch money.) Siegel came into the gang with Suchowljansky. Masseria, a traditional Sicilian and also anti-Semitic, warned Lucania and Doto against Costello, a non-Sicilian inexplicably cozy with the police, and against the two Jews.[21]

The first deal for the new Lucania/Doto gang was an offer from Waxey Gordon, at a Philadelphia boxing match, to sell them ten thousand dollars' worth of quality whiskey for resale. Gordon probably also directed them to Rothstein as their banker. Rothstein advised them not to dilute the liquor but market it at a high price to rich New Yorkers. (Quality alcohol by the mid-1920s was a consumer good on a par with fur coats, fancy cars, and diamond jewelry.) Rothstein also mentored them on the proper suits for businessmen, on the importance of good manners so they could relate to wealthy clients, and how to make decisions based on profitability. Costello had Americanized his name earlier, and now Lucania, Doto, and Suchowljansky Americanized their names—to Charlie "Lucky" Luciano, Joe Adonis, and Meyer Lansky.

This syndicate soon began smuggling its own liquor, first from the Bahamas—with Adonis hiring Bill McCoy telling him there would be millions in it for him—and then from Europe. One of their earliest hauls was in an Azorean ship, which hovered off *Lightship Ambrose* while gang members personally went out in speedboats to unload the liquor, making repeated trips to shore. The Portuguese cook on this ship, interviewed later by federal agents, could only recall their first names—Charlie, Frank, Joe. Charlie would have been Luciano. Frank could have been Costello or Frankie Yale from Brooklyn. Joe would have been Adonis. The gang was a violent one and McCoy quit. Meanwhile Masseria feared he was losing control of Luciano and Adonis, who were becoming increasingly wealthy from smuggling.[22]

While this syndicate grew and expanded, the U.S. District Attorney for Southern New York remained in the dark, too busy focusing on the Irish-American one on the West Side. Asked to appear before a Judiciary subcommittee of the U.S. Senate in 1926, Attorney Buckner commented on the "foreign element" in bootlegging and smuggling in New York City by saying, "It is certainly not so marked that it has become a matter of such comment that it has reached me yet."[23]

Two years later, a man unknown to the public was killed in the streets by hired gunmen in a car with Illinois license plates—New York City's first major gangland assassination. Few knew the dead man was Brooklyn's top bootleg gangster or that he also handled smuggled liquor for Capone in Chicago. New York reporters assigned to the story were surprised to see ten thousand mourners follow the man's hearse, as well as 250 cars, including 38 carrying floral arrangements. The scene at Holy Cross Cemetery when a hundred men, each holding a single rose, simultaneously tossed these onto the coffin as it was lowered into the ground, also amazed reporters except for those familiar with mobster funerals in Chicago. They thought this one in New York compared favorably. The corpse was Frankie Yale.[24]

Almost twenty years earlier, New York City had witnessed an Italian funeral also attended by thousands. That was to honor Joseph Petrosino from the New York Police Department's Italian-speaking detective unit. He was murdered on assignment in Sicily, exploring connections between the mafia and the city's *Unione Sicilione*.[25]

The Broadway Mob

By the mid-1920s, Lower Manhattan's three liquor syndicates, headed by Jewish-Americans, Irish-Americans, and Italian-Americans, had relocated to midtown near Broadway and Times Square. The Knickerbocker Building, once a fancy hotel, was now an office building known as a "warren" of bootleggers. The Prohibition Bureau, realizing the significance of midtown to bootlegging, opened a sting operation called the Bridge and Whist Club at 14 East 44th. This proved short-lived due to negative publicity in Congress about using government funds to run a speakeasy.[26]

The big midtown draw for bootleggers and smugglers was not only that it was the commercial hub for the entire metropolis, but that it provided access to banker Arnold Rothstein, "AR," "The Big Fellow," and "The Man Uptown," who rarely left midtown except for occasional jaunts to the race tracks at Saratoga. Rothstein's midtown business operations included twenty-six holding companies, among these a bail bond business, insurance, and real estate. Most nights, he could be found at his regular table at midtown Lindy's Restaurant popular with newsmen, politicians, gamblers, theater people, and con artists. At Lindy's, he made loans from fifty thousand to one hundred thousand dollars in cash. The Coast Guard suspected Chase National Bank of funding bootleggers like Rothstein who recorded his $10 million in loans in a small, black book kept on his person. When he slept, he hid the book in a stuffed chair in his home. When borrowers repaid, he drew a line through their names and the amount of the loan. If a single payment were missed, he would hound the borrower or send the Diamond brothers to "enforce" quick repayment. Borrowers, both legitimate and underworld figures, were uniformly pressured to patronize his other businesses for bail funds, insurance needs, and to rent rooms and apartments in his buildings and hotels at rates above the market.[27]

A slim man of moderate height, Rothstein dressed like a conservative, successful Manhattan businessman. He pressured borrowers to patronize his Broadway tailor who gave him kickbacks. New York City during Rothstein's "reign" undoubtedly boasted the best-dressed gangsters in America: several owned at least one $250 suit, very expensive for that era. When gangsters gunned down a victim in an Italian-American grocery store in Greenwich Village in the 1920s, onlookers described the killers to police and reporters as well-dressed men wearing pinstriped suits with fedoras pulled down low over their foreheads. Possibly the best-dressed gangster was Larry Fay, the "Beau Brummel of Broadway" who brought back twelve trunks of stylish London clothing after a trip abroad. Rothstein and Fay owned most off-Broadway clip joints where drunken tourists and out-of-town businessmen were pressured into paying bogus bills with personal checks and IOUs.[28]

Rothstein's power and influence extended beyond the underworld into police headquarters, City Hall, and the judiciary. In the late nineteenth century, Tammany bosses used gangs to rig voting returns and then ordered the police to ignore gang activities the rest of the year. A gambling scandal in the early twentieth century exposed these ties between politicians and gangs. After that, Tammany boss Tom Foley, alderman, sheriff, saloonkeeper, district leader, and mentor of Al Smith, began distancing himself from the underworld, relying more and more on Rothstein as his intermediary. Rothstein assumed power as Foley aged. (City courts dismissed six thousand Prohibition cases in the early 1920s, probably at Rothstein's direction.) Politicians honored Foley by naming a square, near the site of his most popular pre-Prohibition saloon, after him following his death in 1925. Foley Square was near City Hall. Rothstein stepped into the power vacuum left by Foley's death.[29]

The *Broadway Mob*, so called because it was based on Broadway in midtown, ruled New York City in the mid-1920s. Its better known gangsters included Rothstein, Fay, Gordon, Dwyer, Diamond, Costello, Luciano, Adonis, and Lansky. The Mob took in an estimated $12 million a year. The group paid $200 a week to one hundred employees in an era when the average store clerk took home $25 a week. In addition, $100,000 a week was paid in graft to police, federal agents, and city magistrates and other court officials. Ten percent of that, or $10,000, was dedicated to top police officers and politicians and carried to City Hall in a paper bag, as if it were lunch, by an Irish-American work-man. The remaining millions were divided among bootleg gangsters. The Broadway Mob was ruling New York City and pocketing millions in the process.[30]

5

SCOFFLAW CITY

Smugglers and bootleggers during Prohibition existed in response to the continuing demand for liquor from scofflaws. New York City had thousands of speakeasies, hundreds of night clubs, and hundreds of thousands of customers drinking at home or in private parties. The *New York Telegram* published a list of places where residents and visitors could buy liquor, including dancing academies, drugstores, delicatessens, cigar stores, soda fountains, shoeshine parlors, barber shops, paint stores, fruit stands, vegetable markets, grocery stores, athletic clubs, boarding houses, Republican and Democratic clubs, and laundries. Bootleggers also had business cards, since they could not advertise in newspapers, for home and office deliveries. Those were made by "businessmen" carrying briefcases. New York City had become Scofflaw City.[1]

Pre-Prohibition liquor, stored before January 1920 in bonded warehouses and private cellars, was legal and could be consumed with a clear conscience: such supplies eventually ran out. Speakeasies were always illegal because they sold liquor. (The name came from English nineteenth-century "speak-softly" establishments, which smuggled liquor to evade taxes.) Night clubs were a new development in the early 1920s and considered legal at first, as long as waiters provided glasses, ice, and ginger ale and customers brought their own liquor from their pre-Prohibition stores. When night clubs began selling liquor, owners, bartenders, and waiters were liable to prosecution under the Volstead Act.

Although drinking per se was not illegal during Prohibition, police and federal agents sometimes needed to be reminded of this. When 150

Figure 5.1. Typical Dock Scene in Scofflaw City
Curious people on the docks stare at beer barrels aboard a seized rumrunner.
Club and speakeasy owners in the crowd wondered how the seizure would
affect the beer supply. Scofflaws wondered how this might affect the price of
beer. Courtesy of the National Archives.

patrons at the Miami Inn in Greenwich Village were arrested for drinking and hauled to the neighboring courthouse, the judge who freed them
admonished the authorities to leave such patrons alone. This case and
others led a prominent Manhattan food critic to remind those planning
a night on the town to take along bail money for emergency use after
they had enjoyed their dinner and before they were served their Chablis.

As long as pre-Prohibition liquor cellars held out, New Yorkers drank
undisturbed at private clubs such as the Harvard Club, Yale Club, and
New York Yacht Club, birthplace of the America's Cup. John McGraw,
manager and part-owner of the New York Giants and friend of State
Senator Jimmy Walker who lobbied to end the ban on Sunday baseball, was involved in a drunken brawl at the Lamb's Club in the early

1920s. The Prohibition Agency was reluctant to bring charges because the fight began at a private club popular with the elite of the theater, arts, and sports world. But this attitude soon changed. A few years later, Rene Le Montagne, a former polo player, sold liquor as the bartender at the exclusive Park Avenue Racquet and Tennis Club which had a tennis court like those used in the days of Louis XIV. Le Montagne was convicted of selling thousands of gallons of wine and hundreds of cases of scotch and sentenced to four years in prison.[2]

Broadway director Earl Carroll was called before a federal grand jury in Manhattan in the early 1920s and asked to name the bootlegger who had supplied champagne for his notorious private after-theater party. At that event, a nude "actress" bathed on stage in a tub filled with champagne while male guests came up on stage to drink from the tub with a dipper. Under oath, Carroll refused to tell the grand jury the name of his bootlegger, insisting that the tub was only filled with ginger ale. Perjury was common in Prohibition cases and U.S. Attorney Emory Buckner decided to make a public example of Carroll and prosecute him for lying. Buckner was successful although many in the city thought the trial a complete circus. The "actress" later profitably re-created the event in the *Greenwich Village Follies*. Manhattan smugglers and pirates, familiar with Broadway events, replicated the party at sea: one pirate put a mop on his head and stepped into a tub filled with champagne. Details of that party are mentioned in Coast Guard records of the interrogation of the ship's cook. (That record does not mention if the pirate in the tub was nude.)[3]

Hotels in Manhattan were not usually raided or padlocked, even if liquor was consumed on the premises. They were too important to the city's tourist economy. Hotel managers disclaimed any responsibility for "private parties." When the the mayor and police commissioner attended the banquet of the Police Lieutenants' Benevolent Association at the Hotel Commodore, no one was arrested although plenty of alcohol was consumed by attendees. They brought it in suitcases, handbags, and paper bags. Ten years into Prohibition, a debutante party of Woolworth heiress Barbara Hutton was held at the Ritz-Carlton. Prior to the party, the Coast Guard began monitoring a yacht in the Upper Bay leased to Norman B. Woolworth, probably suspecting liquor was to be smuggled for the event. When the yacht sailed for the Caribbean, the agency telegraphed to its Washington headquarters, "Assume that the Bird has flown [sic]." The yacht was never stopped or searched. Later, guests consumed two thousand bottles of champagne at the Hutton party, two per guest.[4]

Downtown

The first speakeasies and night clubs opened in lower Manhattan because immigrants in those neighborhoods opposed the 18th Amendment from the outset. They also had access to liquor because the earliest smuggling syndicates were located there.

McSorley's, one of the city's oldest saloons and located in a brick tenement at 15 East Seventh, remained open throughout Prohibition. The saloon replicated the Irish saloon where the original Mr. McSorley worked before emigrating to New York in the mid-nineteenth century. Here homesick, Irish immigrants could imagine that they had never left their country. During Prohibition, Barney Kelly made ale in its basement, diluting it so it could be called *near beer,* yet customers could get drunk on it. The saloon was never raided because police and politicians, mostly Irish, were steady customers. O'Learys on the Bowery also continued operation during Prohibition, giving away thick soup and free floor space for sleeping but charging for liquor. Clients were bums and derelicts but not panhandlers or hobos. "John the Baptist" sometimes played Gershwin and Cole Porter on the piano. Pete's Tavern, 18th and Irving, reputedly where O'Henry wrote "Gift of the Magi" in the second booth, survived Prohibition by disguising itself externally as a "floral shop"—drinking customers entered through a back room and a dummy refrigerator door. Kelly's on Hester Street also remained open and served liquor.[5]

Patrons of Gypsy Night Club, on Second Avenue on the Lower East Side, were from Central Europe. The primary languages spoken in the club were German and Hungarian. The orchestra played ethnic music and the walls were decorated with murals of European mountains and gypsies. Quite different patrons could be found at the 19th Hole, address unknown near Wall Street, where discreet English-speaking waiters served food in private rooms to bond salesmen and customers' wives.

Greenwich Village, with Italian tenements, second-generation Irish, and bohemian rebels from everywhere, was connected to midtown by subway a few years prior to Prohibition. Residents elsewhere in the city, as well as tourists and businessmen visiting midtown, could easily travel by subway to the Village to seek out speakeasies and clubs. John and

Jean's, 139 West 10th Street, required visitors to walk through a Franco-Italian restaurant, climb stairs to the next floor, and then descend in the back. Julius, at #159 on the same street, primarily served Villagers and was named after its popular bartender: here people stood six deep at the bar despite the fact that the beer was heavily needled. Three Steps Down, a cellar club on West Eighth, was managed by Ira Gershwin's in-laws, and his brother George sometimes stopped in to play the piano. Romany Marie's, a pre-Prohibition Turkish coffeehouse, relocated to Washington Square and became a speakeasy for intellectuals, poets, artists, musicians, and anthropologists singing Eskimo songs. No doormen, passwords, or cards were needed at Stonewall's, 91 Seventh Avenue, but visitors needed to know in advance where to find it in a low, quaint building.

The Fronton, 88 Washington Place, was an elegant Village speakeasy popular with poet Edna St. Vincent Millay, State Senator Walker, and reporter Herbert Bayard Swope of the *New York World*. The owners bought directly from Italian bootleggers who obtained liquor smuggled to the docks on the nearby Hudson River. When local gangs tried to shake down the two cousins who owned and operated it, a childhood friend, now a federal agent, brought five other agents to talk with the bullies and discouraged further harassment. This was the second of four speakeasies owned and managed by Jack Kriendler and Charlie Berns. Their first, begun when they were still college students, was the Red Head also in the Village. Kriendler's widowed mother stored their first liquor supplies in her home, and his teenage brother pulled the bottles in a red wagon, camouflaged with groceries, across town from the Lower East Side to the Village. Kriendler said Prohibition agents Izzy Einstein and Moe Smith, from their same East Side neighborhood, never raided the Red Head and sometimes stopped in for a free drink.[6]

The Second Half of the Night, on a dingy, anonymous street in the Village, was quite different from the Fronton. Italian-American patrons walked down a dark hallway, through a padlocked gate, and into a large room painted by local artists. One English tourist obtained admission only after producing a business card from a Harlem undertaker who had written on it that the bearer was a friend. Initially, the man and his date were served only ginger ale for fear they might be federal agents.

The Village also had political and theatrical clubs serving liquor. Sam Schwartz, who ran the Liberal Club at 137 Macdougal Street, closed it and moved across the street to open the Black Knight Club, informally called Sam's with a reputation for excellent liquor. His place was popular with magazine editors, mid-level executives, and dentists but not Village radicals. They were more comfortable at Chumleys, 86 Bedford Street, where Cather, Fitzgerald, and Hemingway reputedly hung out. The place had several entrances and exits including an underground tunnel a block away as well as a secret door behind a bookcase leading to a side alley. It was popular with radicals because owner Lee Chumley published pamphlets and circulars for the International Workers of the World, the "Wobblies." The police seemed more interested in his political activities than in the speakeasy: Chumley was never accused of violating the Volstead Act, but he was once arrested for possessing a penknife. The Triangle, on 11th Street, decorated with news clippings on its walls, had a small stage for occasional theater presentations. By the mid-1920s, one theater critic found its plays inferior and viewed this as a sign of the decay of the Village, blaming it on landlords making it expensive and respectable and, in the process, driving poor, clever, bohemians out.[7]

Don Dickerman's Pirate's Den was on Minetta Lane and later, still in the Village, on Sheridan Square. Dickerman, in his youth the "man-mangling Human Gorilla" at Maine county fairs, recreated a carnival atmosphere in his club: waiters dressed as pirates, there was a talking parrot, and background effects of stormy winds and ships' bells were provided along with murals of pirate scenes. Using cutlasses and pirate slang, the waiters occasionally acted out scenes from *Treasure Island*. In contrast, a nearby club called the Half-Past Nine on Eighth Avenue had neither pirate waiters, nor parrots, nor sound effects and kept its liquor hidden in a large, stuffed bear.

Jo's, located in the basement of a Village tenement, was furnished with chairs, old sofas, and tables. Its patrons were young people and middle-age single men, all interested in the topic of sex. Weekly discussions included the "social position of a gigolo" or the meaning of "sex appeal" about the time Hollywood films were introducing Clara Bow as the "It Girl." There were theatrical presentations with gay patrons giving imitations of "pansies." Lesbians and women experimenting with the lesbian lifestyle danced together in the narrow space between tables.[8]

An unnamed speakeasy in the Village was popular with newsmen and corrupt federal agents. Perhaps its popularity was due to the fact that it was on a street corner and offered seven access doors from both streets, allowing seven exit points. When one door was padlocked by authorities, customers used another. Once six doors were padlocked at the same time, leaving only one door for entry. When the seventh door was finally padlocked, the time limit on at least one other door had conveniently expired, and the speakeasy remained open.[9]

Lower Manhattan, besides having the earliest clubs and speakeasies, was also the first to witness a political protest against the 18th Amendment before it even became law. Wartime Prohibition was still in effect when authorities arrested waiters at the Greenwich Village Inn for serving liquor in 1919. Barney Gallant, its manager, convinced the authorities to allow him to serve prison time instead of his waiters. "Free Barney Gallant" petitions, signed by thousands, were circulated in the Village and eventually elsewhere in Manhattan. The judge agreed to release him for ten days to get his affairs in order and then ordered him back to jail to finish his thirty-day sentence. Afterward, capitalizing on his fame, Gallant opened Club Gallant on Washington Square. He also opened the exclusive Washington Square Club in an elegant, private mansion on the same square.

Midtown

By the mid-1920s, speakeasies and clubs in midtown began to surpass those in the Village in popularity because more middle-class New Yorkers, not just immigrants and ethnic groups, were beginning to scoff at the 18th Amendment.

Most popular pre-Prohibition restaurants in Manhattan were forced to close in the early 1920s because they were unprofitable if they could not serve liquor with dinners. The Cafe des Beaux Arts in midtown remained open, continued to serve good wine with its meals despite the law, and thrived although eventually it was raided. Two streets south was the J and L Club on West 38th where patrons walked up a wobbly staircase to the second floor of a loft building and through a thick fire door to dine on steaks reputedly as thick as telephone books. Of six hundred patrons in evening dress at the Hollywood Club in Times Square, eleven were arrested for having hip flasks. During this raid, a crowd gathered outside to jeer at the agents as those arrested emerged into the street. The Cloud Club on the top floor of the new Chrysler Building was immune from such raids given the opportunity for advanced warning from people on lower floors.

Simplon, a club in a plain exterior in the West 40s, was always difficult to get into: questions were asked at the door and patrons had to answer in a casual or even imperious manner to be admitted. Jack Dunstan's place, on 43rd and Sixth Avenue, was raided twice and $100,000 worth of liquor confiscated before it was closed for good. The Forty-fourth Street Club, 405 West 44th Street on the third floor, was popular with musicians, music publishers, booking agents, and mail order people, and was unlike most dark and dim speakeasies because it had windows on two sides filling it with sunlight. According to one expert, "booze fights" were welcome at this place and the beer was not needled. Some called 45th Street itself, near Broadway, the wettest in the entire country. The first two floors at Dinty Moore's on 46th were popular with theater people as a place to rendezvous. James "Dinty" Moore lived on the third floor and stored liquor on the fourth. At the Pansy Club on Broadway and 48th, female impersonators and a "pansy" chorus entertained a straight crowd. The Silver Slipper, run by Duffy for Fay and Madden, was also on 48th. Tom Shine's Hideaway on 49th was run "incognito" after Shine's earlier club on Seventh Avenue was raided.[10]

Patrick Dennis's semi-autobiographical novel, entitled *Auntie Mame*, is about Marion Tanner, his zany aunt, who lived in the Village during Prohibition. The novel includes a reference to the Aquarium in the West 50s. When Auntie Mame told her young nephew that she was going there with friends while leaving him home, he innocently asked if she would be eating fish. She patiently explained the place was a speakeasy, and he pretended to understand. The Aquarium's bar was on top of a giant, gold-trimmed aquarium. The bar's special was called the "Goldfish" and was equal parts goldwasser, gin, and vermouth.

The Mansion, a speakeasy in a former banker's mansion at 27 West 51st with chandeliers, drapes, and a grand staircase, admitted those with selectively given out "wooden" cards. Less elitist was the speakeasy over a garage on 50th west of Sixth called the Old-Fashioned Club, a hard-drinking establishment popular with horse players, gamblers, the unemployed, and the Broadway fringe. When the beer was terrible, the bartender would dismiss complaints saying it came from a "Bad Barrel," adding that he had to serve what "they" gave him, meaning underworld bootleggers. Every third drink was on the house. The Ship Ahoy, 52 West 51st, was decorated like a tropical island and visitors walked up a gangplank from the sidewalk to the dining room. To get into the bar, they had to say, "The captain sent me." Neighborhood residents, chorus girls, people with a walk-on part on Broadway, and homosexuals—called the *middle sex regiment*—patronized this club.

On one block of West 52nd Street, there were thirty-nine clubs and speakeasies. Mac Kriendler and Robert Benchley, theater critic, visited every club in one night intending to take notes, but gave up documenting after they got hopelessly drunk. The first speakeasy to open on 52nd—Jean Billiams—was in a converted millionaire's mansion. Club 21, the most famous and lasting of Kriendler's and Berns' speakeasies, was at #21 on West 52nd and known informally as "Jack and Charlie's." The Onyx, famed for appealing to musicians, was at #35. Here patrons descended stone steps to a basement door, walked down a short hall, climbed a dark staircase, and walked down a dark hallway to a silver door. A man behind a peephole then asked for the password, rumored to be the name of a famous jazz musician but actually the number of the New York Musicians Local. The Dizzy Club, at 64 West 52nd, had a sign behind the bar with the letters "WYBMADIITY." If a patron asked what it meant, he or she was asked, "Will you buy me a drink if I tell you?" The club's motto was "A rolling tomato gathers no mayonnaise." Little Maison Doree, #72 West 52nd, was popular and issued cards of admission but did not demand these. In fact, the staff was suspicious of anyone who insisted on showing one. The Park Grill at #106 had a nonalcoholic bar at street level: those in the know went upstairs to a barred door and used a password or a special knock to be admitted to the real bar. Photos of Governor Al Smith and Mayor Jimmy Walker were posted on the walls along with a copy of an 1840s liquor license issued to Abraham Lincoln and his Illinois partners. The place was popular with Broadway people, musicians, and song writers.[11]

The Epicure, 40 East 52nd, in a white stone house with thick carpets, featured an African-American orchestra and upscale clientele who liked to read the *Wall Street Journal* and the *Economist*. The short-lived Philanthropic Club, in another mansion on the same street, welcomed poor intellectuals and artists at free or reduced membership and eventually failed for lack of paying customers. A place called Gus, at 112 East 52nd, was popular with the opera and concert crowd and required a card for admission.

The Bath Club, in a three-story mansion at 35 West 53rd, featured gold brocade, a foyer of marble and gold, an elegant dining room, and excellent drinks but no plebeian beer for its svelte and sophisticated patrons. The Silver Mattress, on Park Avenue near 53rd Street, was less sophisticated, and patrons sat or lay about on silver mattresses placed on the floor surrounded by silver walls and curtains. Debutantes, musicians, Broadway chorus girls, and rich Park Avenue residents loved the club. Husbands walking dogs late at night could drop in, with the dogs accommodated in a separate room, until their wives read about this in Walter Winchell's gossip columns and put a stop to it. The club was run by Belle Livingstone who also owned and managed the short-lived Philanthropy Club and the highly successful Country Club, later called the Park Avenue Club, in the same general neighborhood. A tall, long-legged woman who had danced on Broadway in the Gay Nineties, Livingstone was a confident, heavyset individual in her fifties and reputedly acted as her own bouncer, once personally tossing out an entire squad of federal agents. Her club was raided soon after that. Captured in red satin pajamas while fleeing across the club's rooftop, she was sentenced to thirty days in the Women's Prison in Harlem. Earl Carroll, convicted of perjury and imprisoned years earlier for not naming his bootlegger, sent her flowers, and young actor Cary Grant waited outside the prison on the day of her release to escort her home in an armored car, loaned by another night club hostess.[12]

Helen Morgan had several midtown night clubs during Prohibition. A mere twenty years old when she arrived in Manhattan at the start of the era, Morgan sang in many clubs and eventually had two named after her, Chez Morgan and Helen Morgan's Summer Home, both on 52nd Street. She achieved wider fame when she sang two show-stopping songs in *Showboat* when it opened on Broadway. She once spent a night in jail after a raid at one club where agents did $75,000 worth of damage. When she appeared on Broadway the following night, the sympathetic audience spontaneously gave her a round of applause, some shouting out what a shame that she had been arrested. When her next club was raided, she was charged in court as its owner. Government attorneys told the jury a star like Morgan had a particular "duty" to American youth to model good values and not influence them to visit night clubs. She was found not guilty because she never owned any of her clubs: she died a decade later from liver complications.[13]

The Fifty/Fifty Club on 54th stocked up on so much pre-Prohibition liquor that newspapers reported it as an unbonded liquor warehouse. Bill's Bar, 57 East 54th, was an old-fashioned bar with swinging half-doors, silver dollars set in the floor, Currier and Ives prints on the walls, and a cigar-store Indian by the door. The bar was popular with older women and always open. The lively Napoleon Club, in a mansion at 33 West 56th with a hall of mirrors, was patronized by theatrical people, especially from musical comedies. A card was needed to enter unless one was famous or wealthy. Two African-American men pushed a piano about the room from table to table, performing catchy tunes and "porno-parodies" of current hits. There were few dull nights at this club as it was open to the "ridiculous and the bizarre." The entrance to the Cave, between 56th and 57th Street on Sixth Avenue, was down a cellar staircase from the lobby of an apartment building on 57th. That street was widened and the building pushed back seven feet before Prohibition. Thus, customers in this particular speakeasy probably found themselves speaking quite loudly under a sidewalk.[14]

Strollers, a restaurant on East 59th, featured a hidden door in its south wall leading to a speakeasy frequented by gangsters, gamblers, actors down on their luck, construction crews from nearby Radio City, Shriners, and longshoremen. A quite different experience was the Colony Restaurant on 63rd off Madison, which served liquor in demitasse cups. Its liquor was kept in an elevator and sent to the roof in the event of a raid.

One of the last surviving Irish saloons was the Columbus Circle Club in the 60s with a telegraph ticker for the latest sports news, a silent bartender, and hard, fast drinkers who hated the Volstead Act and spat noisily into spittoons. The Irish Veterans' Association near the 69th Street Armory, popular with employees of the National Guard and Bellevue Hospital, had Irish tenors but no Irish whiskey. Instead it served needled beer and second drinks were on the house.

Yorkville's famous pre-Prohibition Zum Brauhaus was at 239 East 86th. During Prohibition, its waiters continued the tradition of handling ten beer steins at a time. The restaurant remained a family place with *Frauen und kinder* welcome, children allowed a sip of beer, and was never raided. According to one expert, authorities knew better than to challenge its popularity in that German neighborhood.

Harlem

Harlem's population in the 1920s made it the nation's largest "black city" within a city. Scofflaws, who began patronizing clubs and speakeasies in lower Manhattan and then moved to midtown, discovered the northern part of Manhattan at the end of the 1920s during the "Harlem

Renaissance" in the arts, music, and literature. Clubs and speakeasies were also part of the Renaissance. Most white scofflaws who journeyed to Harlem were exposed to black culture for the first time. Some Harlem clubs preferred white customers, others favored black patrons, and a few welcomed integrated audiences. (The United States was unofficially segregated in the North and legally segregated in the South during Prohibition.)[15]

The Cotton Club, 644 Lexington Avenue and 142nd, formerly the site of boxing champion Jack Johnson's Club Deluxe, was the most famous Harlem club. Owned by gangsters like Madden, the club was primarily for whites, admitting a few black couples but refusing admittance to most blacks: racially mixed couples were not allowed. With Duke Ellington, Cab Calloway, and Ethel Waters performing, the club's fame spread far beyond New York City with live radio broadcasts of the music. On Sunday nights, major Broadway actors and actresses showed up at the club to take bows and, sometimes, to perform.

Connie's Inn, 132nd Street and Seventh Avenue, was another stop for white clubbers. Entertainer Jimmy Durante called it the swankiest place in Harlem with its classy outside red canopy, high prices inside, and waiters cautioning customers to keep bottles in their pockets and not on the floor. Brothers Connie and George Immerman, who owned the place and squeezed 125 couples inside, refused admittance to "mixed parties," but admitted a few black couples. According to the *Daily News*, the club lacked a Harlem atmosphere and was merely a black version of midtown white clubs. There was a gunfight outside Connie's one night. Two bystanders were injured and a Harlem society woman killed.

Baron Wilkins' Exclusive Club was popular with whites, including Southerners reputedly "nostalgic" for black society. The club was also popular with African-American sporting men and leaders. White and black couples shared tables, but working-class African-Americans were unwelcome. The Nest, 169 West 133rd, was popular with white women who supposedly ogled Dickie Wells, its handsome proprietor. This club was the first in Harlem to be padlocked, although clubs had been padlocked downtown and in midtown years earlier. This delay was probably less due to racism, not caring about Harlem clubs or thinking they were worth padlocking, than to the fact that few prominent clubs existed in Harlem until the late 1920s.[16]

Small's Paradise, 135th in Harlem, was owned and operated by African-American Ed Small. It had one of the best floor shows and bands in the city and was "the hottest spot in Harlem" for jazz with fifteen hundred patrons flocking there to listen or dance. Waiters sometimes danced the Charleston while carrying trays to and from the kitchen. Blacks and whites, looking for genuine black music and entertainment, were always welcome. Langston Hughes, who lived nearby at East 127th, wrote a short story, "Who's Passing for Whom," about a midwestern white couple and their black escort at Small's. When the escort told them light-skinned blacks sometimes passed for white, they "confessed" to being black, fooled him, and succeeding in having him show them the real Harlem, a richer experience than most whites had. Carl Van Vechten visited the club while researching his novel *Nigger Heaven* (1926) set in Harlem. Blacks found his title offensive and he was unwelcome at the club after its publication. Ethel Waters, who initially objected to the title, eventually concluded he knew more about Harlem than any white man except the captain of the Harlem police station. (Van Vechten chose the title from a contemporary theater term for segregated balconies, believing that Harlem was such a balcony overlooking the white theater that was the rest of Manhattan.)[17]

Edmond's Cellar at 132nd and Fifth Avenue, where gamblers, hookers, and underworld types gathered, was mentioned in court records as a place of "race mixing." About two hundred people could fit inside the club whose walls were covered with photographs of black boxers and entertainers. Ex-boxer "Mississippi," the only black licensed to drive a horse hack through Central Park, brought wealthy "white slumming parties" to this club and entertained them with his dancing.[18]

Harlem millionaire Casper Holstein financed the Lenox Club and hired Jeff Blount as manager. Everyone was welcome—blacks, whites, and mixed parties—and people danced together on the crowded floor. The club was known for its early Monday morning breakfast dances, which began at four A.M. when black entertainers from downtown shows and other clubs arrived to relax and perform in return for free liquor and food. These jamming sessions ended at eight when customers rushed from the club to start work.

Whites wanting an "authentic" black experience visited the Sugar Cane near 135th, primarily a black club with a low ceiling, worn plank floor, kitchen chairs, and "rickety" tables. One tourist said whites visiting the club might find themselves dancing with their maids or elevator operators. Technically speaking, the Savoy Ballroom at 596 Lenox Avenue was neither a night club nor a speakeasy as its bar provided soft drinks and setups, and patrons brought their own liquor. (Later on, liquor was probably served.) African-American Charles Buchanon managed it. When it opened in the middle of Prohibition, it was one of the first integrated public places for dancing. Every night, for six months, black writer George Schuyler courted his white fiancee at the Savoy: he thought interracial couples were good for New York and for the United States. (After Prohibition, the Lindy Hop, Stomp, and Jitterbug originated here.)

Pyle's Club at 138 on Fifth Avenue, managed by Harry Pyle, served middle-class blacks. Mike's, in the 140s on Seventh Avenue, managed by a black with a white bartender, had a policy of tolerating but not encouraging whites. The message was emphasized by differing drink prices based on race: whites paid a quarter for a drink and blacks paid a dime for the same purchase. After the three A.M. city curfew, patrons moved to a cellar annex two doors down where the bar was made from packing cases pushed together, glasses were unwashed, and patrons could hit their heads on pipes hanging from the ceiling: they tolerated the inconvenience because the place had hot piano-playing, good singers, and risqué songs. Ethel Waters said the nearby Banks' Club, on 133rd Street between Lenox and Fifth, was another "low-down" night club. Harlem's "fast set" hung out at Casper Holstein's Turf Club on 111 West 126th where Holstein ran a numbers racket.

Speakeasies in Harlem were sometimes located in residential buildings. Occasionally, residents opened apartments to the public to raise money to pay the rent. These "rent" parties offered food, live music, dancing, and homemade gin and whiskey.

Dangers for Scofflaws

Scofflaws, those "scoffing" at the law by drinking in clubs and speakeasies in the Village, Midtown, or Harlem, could suffer serious harm if they accidentally chose ones patronized by gangsters or in which they had a major investment.

The Backstage, above a garage on West 56th, was one such club. Waxey Gordon, drinking there one night, knocked a "harmless drunk" to the floor and proceeded to kick him in the head. Billy Rose, owner and manager of this club, watched in horror, ran sobbing back to the kitchen, and sold the club the very next day.[19]

Many clubs had violent confrontations between gangsters, some were extreme, and a few involved well-known people or mobsters. At the Blossom Health Club on 57th, Vinnie Higgins pressured the owner to order beer from his gang and was knifed instead. Casablanca owner Larry Fay was murdered by a disgruntled doorman whose pay had been reduced due to the Depression. Joey Noe, partner of Dutch Schultz, was assassinated at the Chateau Madrid. A man was shot and stabbed at the Club Abbey on 54th. The Club Chantee, run by the Whittemore mob, was deliberately destroyed by fire. Frank Wallace was murdered on the doorstep of La Vie, and it was then closed. A gangster club on 53rd was bombed. Three people, including the bartender, were murdered at Porky Murray's Club on West 52nd. The Plantation Club in Harlem was destroyed within a week of its opening for stealing Cab Calloway away from the Cotton Club. Baron Wilkins was murdered in front of his club in Harlem by a liquor supplier named "Yellow Charleston." Then, there was the infamous Mingo's at 167 East Fourth where police and gangsters would meet to fix cases and to arrange police escorts for liquor convoys.

The Hotsy-Totsy Club, 1721 Broadway between 54th and 55th and owned by Hymie Cohen fronting for Legs Diamond, was an infamous Manhattan club. Two patrons were shot in a drunken brawl here one night while the bandleader ordered the orchestra to play "Alexander's Ragtime Band" loudly to drown out the gunfire. Twenty-five people witnessed the shooting, but no one would admit to seeing anything. Diamond disappeared from the city for eight months and only returned once two witnesses were silenced by death, two others assumed dead, and one permanently missing. The case was never solved.

Most scofflaws managed to avoid gangster clubs and speakeasies but could be seduced into visiting a club like the Rendezvous, which seemed safe enough. That club's hostess eventually admitted her role was to get customers so drunk they could be easily fleeced: it was actually an upscale "clip joint."

Night clubs in midtown hired detective Johnny Broderick for protection. A retired boxer, he refused on principle to carry a gun and stationed himself on the sidewalk outside Lindy's and awaited calls for help. When Legs Diamond began trashing a nearby club whose owner refused to buy "protection," Broderick arrived, beat up Diamond, and warned him to leave the city. Diamond swore revenge and did not leave Manhattan. When Broderick was informed that Diamond was still in the city watching a movie in a certain Broadway theater, Broderick invited Mayor Walker and the Police Commissioner to stand across the street and watch. Then he went inside the theater and emerged holding the tuxedoed Diamond high off the ground, walked over to the nearest alley garbage can, and dumped him in it. When Broderick rejoined his audience of two, they asked why he hadn't arrested Diamond, and the detective replied that clever lawyers would get the gangster released, whereas this incident might shame him into leaving the city.[20]

Besides hiring private detectives, some speakeasies and clubs hired perceptive doormen. Sherman Billingsley, a member of a Western boot-legging gang before he arrived in New York City to run a pharmacy dis-pensing illegal "medicinal" liquor, started the Stork Club on West 58th Street. It foundered until Frank Costello stopped by to leave $100,000 for "safekeeping" while he went abroad. Billingsley soon learned this "loan" came with a price, that his legitimate business partner was front-ing for Madden, Dwyer, and Frenchy de Magne from the Phoenix Cereal Company who then pressured him to buy liquor from them. During the Beer Wars, Billingsley was kidnapped and held for ransom in Harlem before being released. After that he offered to buy Madden and the oth-ers out. They told him they did not own stock that he could repurchase, that they actually owned him for the rest of his life. Nevertheless, his second Stork Club at East 51st was free of gangster influence because he hired a doorman whose major claim was that he knew every gangster by sight. Billingsley told him to keep out everyone he knew.[21]

While scofflaws might succeed in avoiding clubs and speakeasies run by or backed by gangsters, few could be confident of avoiding the danger of unsafe liquor. One New York newspaper collected four hundred liquor samples throughout the city and submitted these to a chemist. Most samples proved to be watered liquor—scofflaws paying lots of money and being cheated, but a significant portion was poisonous, which was understandable in an unregulated, illegal market. A few Prohibition agents even reported finding cooking and fermenting vats in tenement basements with dead rats, mice, and cockroach carcasses floating on top. Rich New York party givers protected themselves by hiring chemists to certify their liquor. Others drank only at places known for quality. After a night on the town, scofflaws could never be entirely sure they hadn't been poisoned until they awoke from hangovers the next morning. Even then they could not be entirely sure: Dorothy Parker checked into the hospital thinking that she had been poisoned by bad liquor, only to learn she had appendicitis. One "Roaring Twenties" Manhattan visitor summed up the era's dangers saying, "Speak easy, Die badly."[22]

Excessive drinking became the norm in New York City during Prohibition. One writer carefully listed more than 100 words or phrases popularly used in the 1920s to describe various stages of inebriation. These included: the jumps; the shakes; the zings; the heebie-jeebies; the screaming-meemies; the whoops; the jingles; as well as to burn with a low blue flame. A new pastime was to trick heavy-drinking friends into thinking they might be in the final stages of Delirium Tremens, commonly called the "DTs." Ring Lardner was drunk at a midtown dinner party in a building adjacent to a Manhattan night club then featuring an act with a python. His hosts borrowed the python and placed it in Lardner's lap. The other guests pretended it wasn't there when he finally became aware of it. Writer Dorothy Parker, drinking with friends in a country home, saw rats run through the room while her hosts pretended not to see them.[23]

New Yorkers, tourists, and visiting businessmen out for a night on the town during Prohibition could successfully avoid the dangers of gangster speakeasies and/or bad liquor by patronizing the Salvation Army's Temperance Saloon in the Hotel Argonne on West 47th. But it would be a tame affair. There would be no raids, no arrests, no gangsters, and no bootleggers. The choices for liquid refreshment would all be legal—coffee, tea, ginger ale, or buttermilk.

6

REPEAL

The continued consumption of liquor throughout the years of Prohibition demanded reconsideration of the 18th Amendment. Repealing a constitutional amendment would be unprecedented in the nation's history. On the other hand, smugglers, bootleggers, and scofflaws behaved as if the amendment did not exist. A political consensus was needed to legalize the use of liquor for personal enjoyment. Scofflaw City produced leaders for that effort, and a 21st Amendment (known as "Repeal") was introduced in the Hundred Days of the New Deal Congress and ratified at the end of 1933.

Leadership in Congress and the New York Legislature

Two politicians from New York City argued against the 18th Amendment before it was ratified. They were Congressman Fiorello La Guardia and State Senator James J. Walker. Throughout Prohibition, they remained opposed and spoke against it: initially, La Guardia did not publicly flout the law, but Walker patronized trendy speakeasies and clubs.

La Guardia became the nation's first Italian/Jewish-American to serve in the U.S. Congress when he won an election in 1916 in the 14th Congressional District in lower Manhattan. Standing five feet tall and heavyset, he often wore a large Stetson hat signifying that, although born in Manhattan, he was raised on an army post in the American West. He spoke against the 18th Amendment when it was first considered insisting it was directed at U.S. cities, particularly ethnic, urban Americans. He predicted it could never be enforced and that it would eventually produce contempt for all law. From 1922 to 1933, he represented East Harlem's 20th Congressional District which had twenty-seven nationalities although it was primarily Italian and Jewish. One of his biographers later claimed that La Guardia did more than any other member of Congress to challenge Prohibition.[1]

Walker, the dapper lawyer from Greenwich Village, was proud of his Irish-American roots. His maternal grandfather, immigrant James Roon, owned a popular, pre-Prohibition saloon in the Village. Walker's immigrant father was a Tammany ward leader, city alderman, and state assemblyman. Senator Walker represented urban Irish-Americans who viewed the repression of saloons under the 18th Amendment as an attack on the Irish-dominated Tammany Hall political machine, which used neighborhood saloons as political organizing centers. When the issue of ratification of the 18th came before the New York Senate, Walker predicted the proposed amendment would fail, that it was an act of bigotry. He said that the real drunkenness in the world was the recent war where nations feasted on the blood of millions of young soldiers. When the 18th Amendment became law, Walker sought to weaken it with passage of the Walker-Gillette Act legalizing beer, but that new law was soon nullified by the U.S. Supreme Court.[2]

The New York City Police Department (NYPD), more than 15,000 strong in the 1920s, was unenthusiastic, even antagonistic, toward Prohibition. When federal agents raided Flanagan Brothers' Restaurant on Grand Street, police officers were there drinking whiskey and beer with their lunches. The 750 policemen, told to sit in cafés throughout the city and watch for liquor violations, hated the assignment, convinced it was a waste of time. When the police conducted a raid, it was often pro forma. One at Little Italy's Sawdust Inn, a stone's throw from police headquarters, was a case in point. It began with a rattle at the door. Ten patrolmen entered single file, clubs swinging from belted waists. Looking neither to the right nor the left, they marched to the kitchen in the rear, reappeared a few minutes later, and marched out as they had entered. The owner then chuckled, raised his glass in a toast to his patrons, and said, "Raid!" Sometimes police found themselves on the receiving end of public rage. During one raid at Peter's Blue Hour on West 48th, angry diners threw hard dinner rolls, wet spaghetti, and even chairs at the police.[3]

Senator Walker became a natural spokesperson for the NYPD's dislike of Prohibition. In 1921, the New York legislature passed the Mullan-Gage Act requiring state and local police actively to enforce Prohibition. Two years later, Walker led a successful fight (by one vote) to repeal it; Governor Smith wavered but eventually signed it. Henceforth, police intervention was required only if a serious crime, like robbery, kidnapping, or murder, was also being committed, or in cases of complaints that clubs or speakeasies were a "public nuisance."

Taking police out of active enforcement in New York State was a serious blow to the Dry cause, which expected and counted on local and state enforcement. The Prohibition Bureau had two thousand agents for the entire country, less than two hundred for New York City with a population in the millions. These agents also had to monitor legal distilleries, denaturing plants, drugstores, doctors, and religious institutions as well as clubs and speakeasies. Making matters worse, agents at the start were political appointees not subject to the Civil Service, making them more easily corruptible. Dry supporters ignored this underfunding, understaffing, and politicizing of the Prohibition Bureau because they naively expected Americans to police themselves. In his first year, New York State's Prohibition Director realized his task was impossible and resigned.[4]

Conflict between the New York Police Department and federal agents was a fact of life during Prohibition. Conflict was exacerbated by pervasive corruption in the ranks. Federal agents raided the Place, in the 40s off Sixth Avenue, so often that some wondered why they repeatedly targeted that speakeasy. Did federal agents carry a grudge against city patrolmen who passively watched as bootleggers rolled beer barrels from trucks, parked in the street, into the speakeasy?[5]

Democratic Party delegates, convened at Madison Square Garden for their national presidential nominating convention in the summer of 1924, included some from states whose police actively enforced Prohibition, and these delegates relished hearing on the floor of Congress from New York representatives that the city would be "wide-open" during the convention, meaning open for drinking. That convention became the longest on record, with more than one hundred ballots between a Dry candidate and a Wet one (Governor Smith) before settling on a dark-horse candidate who lost to Coolidge that fall.

The next year, Emory Buckner became the newly appointed U.S. Attorney for the Southern District of New York. He found Prohibition had created a disrespectful atmosphere in his federal courthouse in Manhattan, now home to "a seething mob of bartenders, peddlers, waiters, bond runners, fixers." Congressman La Guardia, sole Wet on the House Committee on the Alcohol Liquor Traffic, warned the nation that smuggling and bootlegging were becoming highly commercial, spawning a thriving underworld, and suggested that this would be impossible without corruption of government authorities responsible for enforcement. When the U.S. Senate Subcommittee on the Judiciary invited Buckner to Washington, he addressed the issue of Prohibition enforcement in New York City and said, "It has never been tried by the Federal Government in my judgment in my district, not only during my term of office, but before my term of office."[6]

Buckner changed the status quo by enforcing the law more aggressively, not focusing on small-time violators, like waiters and bartenders, but on club owners by raiding and padlocking high-profile and hugely popular midtown clubs and restaurants. He hoped that the financial losses would discourage owners. Newspapers reported Buckner planned to dry up the city in sixty days. But owners simply relocated given the continued demand of the public for night clubs and speakeasies. He identified two large-scale smuggling syndicates, Gordon's on the East Side and Dwyer's on the West, and began building conspiracy cases. Unlike Buckner, La Guardia was not hopeful the law could be enforced, insisting that this would be possible only if the enforcement of Prohibition were the largest item in the federal budget, employing 250,000 agents. He was convinced that most Americans would oppose such a budget. On the other hand, Drys took comfort in a reorganization requiring the Prohibition Bureau, Customs, and the Coast Guard to report to Brigadier General Lincoln C. Andrews, the new Assistant Secretary of the Treasury.[7]

New York City Votes for Repeal

State Senator Walker was elected Mayor of the City of New York in the fall of 1925. Voters knew of his long-standing opposition to Prohibition and seemed to approve. The following fall, New York State held a referendum on the 18th Amendment, and New York City voters overwhelmingly opposed it. Realizing that this made his job, enforcing the Volstead Act, impossible, Buckner resigned. Charles Tuttle, his successor, famously declared that he would never be the first server in a

Prohibition case. So by the mid-1920s, neither the NYPD nor the U.S. Attorney actively enforced Prohibition.[8]

Walker soon became a symbol of opposition to Prohibition, admired throughout the nation as *the* Jazz Age Mayor. He had a colorful personality, loved the limelight, played Tin Pan Alley songs on the piano, dressed stylishly, and thoroughly enjoyed the city's nightlife. There was a small speakeasy under the "very eaves" of City Hall, but Walker chose to patronize more public venues. A late-rising mayor, he spent little time at City Hall but could be found many evenings, when not on frequent trips out of town vacationing or traveling, at the Central Park Casino on West 66th. He was there so much that it was considered, unofficially, the second City Hall. Technically liquor was not served, only setups. When Walker's Police Commissioner became entangled in a power struggle with New York's Prohibition Bureau over drinking at this Casino, Governor Roosevelt summoned him to Albany and insisted he defer to federal authority. He resigned. Federal agents then raided the Casino and arrested nine, leading to a great public outcry as some "very nice" people were involved. Then the Prohibition Bureau Chief was ousted. There is no information stating that the mayor was present during that raid, although he might have been escorted out before people were arrested, as was the case in a raid at another night club where several gay customers were arrested for possessing powder puffs.[9]

Another favorite Walker haunt was the new Club 21 on 52nd Street where the city's social and political elite dined and drank with impunity. The married mayor had a private booth where he and a Broadway dancer could dine undisturbed. The club had police protection, but owners Kriendler and Berns understood there could be no protection from federal raids. When journalist Walter Winchell was refused admittance because of the club's policy to exclude the press, he retaliated on his radio show and in his newspaper column noting the exclusive Club 21 had never been raided. In the ensuing federal raid, $100,000 worth of liquor was seized. After that costly raid, the owners took elaborate precautions to anticipate a future one. The doorman had four different alarm buttons. The bartender could push a button to make the bar slide into a recess in the wall, making glasses and bottles slide down a chute and land unbroken in the basement sandpit. In addition, an elaborate two-ton fake cellar door, of the same material and thickness as the cellar walls, was built to protect stored liquor. A second raid was triggered by publicity when a theater critic was quoted in the press as favoring

Kriendler and Berns for U.S. President and Vice-President because they ran a thriving, satisfying business. The raid lasted twelve hours as agents rapped on walls, measured closets, and stomped around. When they returned to their cars, they found city police had given them parking tickets, one small gesture of support for the club's owners.[10]

In June 1928, Governor Al Smith was nominated in Houston at the Democratic Convention. Later that night Assistant U.S. Attorney General Mabel Walker Willebrandt, a Republican appointee, ordered raids on eleven night clubs and thirty-six restaurants. These raids were in midtown, between 40th and 53rd streets, in the early morning hours when New Yorkers were still celebrating Smith's nomination. The raids publicized to voters throughout the United States that in Manhattan, birthplace of the Democratic candidate, federal liquor laws were openly flouted. During the presidential campaign, Smith spoke out for the right of states to define acceptable alcohol content, although his party's platform took no stand on Prohibition. Republican candidate Herbert Hoover was solidly behind Prohibition. A Republican whisper campaign claimed that Smith drank several cocktails a day, that Mrs. Smith was alcoholic, and that if the Catholic candidate were elected president, he would invite the Pope to live in one wing of the White House.[11]

On election eve November 1928, Arnold Rothstein was at Lindy's anticipating making $200,000 from bets on Hoover over Smith. The gambler needed a big win as he had recently lost $320,000 in a two-day, nonstop Broadway poker game and had yet to pay up. About ten o'clock, he received a phone call and left the restaurant to meet someone. A short while later, he was found lying in the alley of the nearby Park Central Hotel on Seventh Avenue. He had been shot. He regained consciousness in the hospital, made a new will, but refused to talk with police before his death. Mayor Walker, at a suburban night club when he heard of the murder, told an associate this meant trouble: a thorough official investigation would expose ties between the Mob and Walker's administration. The ensuing "investigation" left unanswered questions.[12]

News of Hoover's victory was flashed from Times Square's relatively new, moving, electric, five-foot-high sign. Except for farmers, the nation was in the midst of prosperity. In fact, Drys insisted this prosperity was because a sober workforce was increasingly productive. In retrospect, anti-Catholic prejudice contributed more to Hoover's victory than public opposition to Smith's idea for modification of Prohibition: the nation was not yet ready to elect a Catholic to the presidency and wouldn't be

Figure 6.1. Presidential Election of 1928
The *Al Smith*, a rumrunner registered in Honduras, was named to honor the only avowedly Wet presidential candidate in the era of Prohibition. Courtesy of the National Archives.

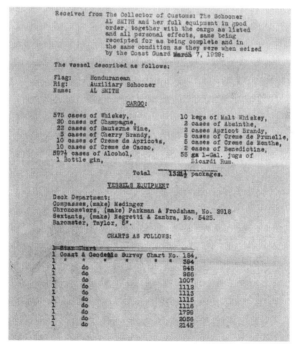

Figure 6.2. Liquor Inventory of the *Al Smith*
Courtesy of the National Archives.

for thirty-two more years. Smith had to console himself with heading the company constructing the new Empire State Building.[13]

One of the last acts of Congress under Coolidge was to pass the Jones Law increasing penalties in Prohibition cases. As the tenth anniversary of the 18th Amendment approached, Hoover named distinguished citizens to a commission to assess Prohibition and asked George Wickersham, retired U.S. Attorney General and partner in a Manhattan law firm, to head the commission. Hundreds of Americans were interviewed and crime statistics collected by the Wickersham Commission, which also visited seized liquor warehouses in Manhattan. When the Commission published five volumes of its findings, scofflaws expected a recommendation to repeal the 18th Amendment and were stunned with a recommendation, instead, for stronger enforcement which would increase the federal budget in the midst of the Great Depression. President Hoover had been advised privately that he could not be in favor of Repeal given his presidential oath of office to uphold the Constitution. So, the recommendation of his presidential commission was a foregone conclusion. In addition, Hoover had to work with a Congress with 80 Dry senators and 328 Dry representatives, a clear majority in both House and Senate.[14]

La Guardia insisted that it was time to end the "farce" of Prohibition, that the law needed to change, and he noted that human beings had been drinking liquor as long as recorded history. "If Prohibition is not creating a temperate, abstaining people, then it is not a success. . . . We must face the situation and do the next thing, admit its failure and so change the law as to meet the views and desires, habits, and customs of a vast majority of the people of this country."[15]

In December 1929, as the tenth anniversary of Prohibition approached, three smugglers were killed by the Coast Guard off the southern New England coast in a boat named the *Black Duck*. La Guardia was incensed and said Americans did not like sailors dying so people could drink. That same month, a New York City magistrate was robbed at gunpoint at a private banquet. In the ensuing publicity, the public learned several gangsters were among the invited guests. The New York State legislature began an investigation into New York City asking retired state judge Samuel Seabury to be lead investigator. The patrician judge, descended from Mayflower passengers and a long line of Episcopal church leaders, brought credibility to the proceeding. Slowly and methodically, he began questioning 175 witnesses and amassing 47,000 pages of testimony.

Rothstein's murder, the *Black Duck* incident, the midnight banquet, the Seabury Investigations, and the Wickersham Commission contributed to a growing public interest in ending Prohibition. The Stock Market crash and the Great Depression, where unemployment reached 25 percent, dealt a blow to Manhattan's nightlife with a sharp decline in the number of night clubs and speakeasies. The Depression also contributed to increased violence within the underworld as gangsters fought over control of declining markets. In New York City, there was a Beer War as rivals hijacked each other's trucks in the streets. Five children playing near 107th Street in East Harlem were wounded in one shootout, and five-year-old Michael Vengalli was killed. Public outrage was intense and not assuaged when "Mad Dog" Coll, the gangster accused of the shooting, was found not guilty thanks to a skilled defense lawyer. The Broadway Mob then deflected some of this public anger by hiring hit men to kill Coll in a drugstore phone booth on West 23rd, raking the booth with machine gunfire while Coll was deliberately kept on the phone talking to Owney Madden. Legalizing real beer was the obvious answer to the Beer War, and ten thousand New Yorkers, some estimate ten times that number, marched in a Protest Parade around Central Park demanding the return of real beer. Mayor Walker, usually late for all engagements arrived ten minutes late and walked in front of the parade.[16]

There was also a deadly struggle within the underworld, out of the public eye, in the early 1930s. Mafia leader Masseria was challenged for power by newcomer Salvatore Maranzano, a recent immigrant from Castellammare in Sicily. Within the underworld, this struggle was known as the Castellammarese War because many of Maranzano's supporters were immigrants from his hometown. Fascist dictator Mussolini's efforts to rid Sicily of the Mafia forced an unusually large number to emigrate, legally or illegally, to the United States on the "Mussolini Shuttle" in the 1920s. Maranzano was the most powerful of these and supposedly was paving the way for top Don Vito Cascia Ferro to emigrate, but Mussolini caught and imprisoned Ferro before that happened.[17]

In this Underworld War, the Broadway Mob emerged triumphant. Luciano and friends first allied themselves with newcomer Maranzano and assassinated Masseria in a deserted Coney Island restaurant. A few months later, they hired Jewish hit men, posing as federal tax agents, to murder Maranzano in his office in the New York Central Building. Luciano and Lansky also began eliminating future rivals within the

Broadway Mob, neutralizing Waxey Gordon by leaking financial documents to the government to prove him guilty of tax evasion, the same charge that felled Capone in Chicago. Gordon, despite his millions or because of them, went to prison. Madden assessed the situation and left to open a vacation spa and hideaway in Hot Springs, Arkansas.

Manhattan Residents as National Leaders

Dr. Nicholas Murray Butler, president of Columbia University, was keenly aware that drinking on college campuses had increased under Prohibition: college students found that they could rebel against the older generations simply by drinking. Only 5 percent of Americans attended college before World War II, making this population an elite group of future leaders. Butler and La Guardia were both troubled that these students were learning disrespect for the law. In fact, La Guardia told Congress that he would have considered Prohibition successful if it had the "wholehearted support on the part of the younger generation." Instead, a majority of college students "developed an appetite for synthetic gin, raw hooch, or anything they can get their hands on." One Harvard student agreed, noting that many drank in the dorms, in fraternity and sorority houses, at roadhouses and weekend parties, and in the rumble seats of cars. He said the quality of the liquor was terrible although the quantity consumed was great.[18]

Many speakeasies and clubs in Manhattan catered to collegians. The Metamora Club, popular with Yale and Princeton undergraduates, was raided. Jack's, 88 Charles Street, in Greenwich Village was patronized by Columbia students. The nearby Red Head was popular with students from Columbia and New York University. The Kinvara Cafe, 381 Park Avenue, advertised in college newspapers and kept its liquor supply in the pockets of an enormous overcoat worn by a person standing on the customers' side of the bar: he would hand bottles across to the bartender as needed and walk out with the students in the event of a raid. The Biarritz, on East 52nd, was raided after a Prohibition agent, pretending to be a college student, was served. The Puncheon Club, 42 West 49th, in an iron-gated brownstone, was especially popular with Yale undergraduates and alumni because it was located in the basement of what had been the childhood home of Yale undergraduate Ben Quinn. (In fact, the club was informally known as "Ben Quinn's Kitchen.") The Jungle Room was not a night club but a room designated for use by collegians, within the Country Club on East 58th. It was "rough, noisy, and primitive," according to one critic, and that might explain why Al Capone seemed to prefer it when he visited the club.[19]

Pauline Morton Sabin, daughter of Teddy Roosevelt's Secretary of the Navy and wife of a Manhattan banker, joined Butler in criticizing the 18th Amendment. She founded the Women's National Republican Club and was the first woman to serve on the Republican National Committee. Following Hoover's election, she resigned to found the non-partisan Women's Organization for National Prohibition Repeal (WON-PR). Its goal was to educate the public that enforcement fell unfairly on the middle and working classes, and that Prohibition contributed to a growing disrespect for all laws. The new organization quickly grew from 17 members in 1929 to 1,325,000 in 1932, with housewives, industrial workers, office workers, and business and professional women across the nation among its members.[20]

Histories of the 1920s give the false impression that all women were "flappers" wearing shorter skirts, bobbing their hair, smoking, drinking, and wildly dancing the Charleston. On the other hand, an increasing number of U.S. women patronized speakeasies and night clubs. Sometimes efforts were made to attract them with attention to interior decorating, hiring handsome bartenders, and offering cocktails along with beer and hard liquor. The media enthusiastically covered the WONPR and depicted its members as energetic and modern in their support for Repeal. *Time* gave Sabin the status of a celebrity by featuring her on its cover in July 1932.[21]

A few old-fashioned saloons in Manhattan persisted in refusing women as customers during Prohibition. The most famous was McSorley's which posted two signs—"Good ale, raw onions, no Ladies" and "No Back Room in Here for Ladies." An anonymous feminist from Greenwich Village tried to integrate McSorley's during Prohibition by dressing in trousers, wearing a long overcoat, tucking her hair under a man's hat, and possibly smoking a cigar. He/She went to the bar, ordered, was served, and downed the beer. Then she took off her hat and tossed her hair about while bartender Bill McSorley jumped up and down in angst and sputtered that he had served a woman! (Sued for sexism by

Figure 6.3. Leader of Women for Repeal
Pauline Morton Sabin, leader of U.S. women supporting repeal of the 18th Amendment, appeared on *Time* magazine's cover, July 18, 1932. Courtesy of *Time Magazine*.

feminists in the 1960s Women's Movement, the saloon opened its doors to women August 10, 1970.)[22]

The fight for Repeal gained a significant Republican supporter in June of 1932 when John D. Rockefeller Jr., who lived in a mansion on West 54th, spoke up on its behalf. Rockefeller was a force in the city as Standard Oil Trust's headquarters were in lower Manhattan, Rockefeller Center was under construction in midtown, and the Rockefeller Foundation was a nationally recognized philanthropy. He and his father originally supported the 18th Amendment with contributions and both personally abstained from alcohol. Rockefeller was probably inclined to change his stance by fellow Republicans Butler and Sabin. He may also have read and taken to heart the information in the *Wickersham Report*. His college-aged sons may also have influenced him as there is an unsubstantiated rumor that they took him on a tour of speakeasies and clubs and pointed out that many of these were on Rockefeller-owned land. Belle Livingstone, hostess of the posh Country Club, claimed that Rockefeller attended her opening night, possibly to experience a night club firsthand.[23]

Franklin Delano Roosevelt was the last New York leader to support Repeal. Privately, he was rumored to enjoy a good martini. Eleanor Roosevelt initially supported Prohibition as her father died in his twenties from alcoholism. Sarah Delano Roosevelt, the matriarch, maintained that Prohibition was designed to close saloons and not to deny those who wanted French wine with dinner. As governor, Roosevelt needed to be on good terms with rural and upstate New York voters and remained unconvinced that they supported Repeal, even if sophisticated urban New Yorkers like La Guardia, Walker, Smith, Butler, Sabin, and Rockefeller did.[24]

The Broadway Mob realized Prohibition would soon end. Costello believed that Americans liked to gamble even more than they liked to drink. He had 5,000 slot machines installed in night clubs throughout New York City. He paid police to leave his machines alone and to seize those of his rivals. Lansky explored investing in gambling in Havana, Cuba, and eventually in Las Vegas. Luciano and Adonis concentrated on traditional mafia concerns within the city, including prostitution and narcotics. But the Mob still needed influence with the police, courts, and the Walker administration and did not want Walker ousted or city government cleaned up.

So the Mob sent an unofficial delegation of two to the Democratic Convention in Chicago in June 1932 to use their influence over New York City Tammany delegates and force Governor Roosevelt to halt the Seabury Investigations, which had snared Walker that May. Luciano shared a room at the convention with Little Italy's delegate Albert Marinelli Jr., and Costello shared a room with the West Side's James J. Hines. If Luciano's memoir is to be believed—a big if—the two gangsters thought they had an understanding with FDR, through an intermediary, that if they threw their support his way he would call off Seabury. (That fall, an intermediary approached Hoover's vice-president, offering to throw the election and was told to "get lost." So, Roosevelt was probably also approached earlier in June.) Ex-Governor Al Smith controlled a majority of New York delegates. He still harbored hopes for the presidential nomination and was slated to speak to the convention about Repeal. Fifteen minutes before Smith took the podium, word spread through the convention hall that FDR would finally support Repeal. He won the nomination and continued to support the Seabury Investigations, insisting on and receiving Mayor Walker's resignation.[25]

Following Roosevelt's landslide election in November of 1932, the 21st Amendment was introduced in the first Hundred Days of the famous New Deal Congress. A bill to modify the Volstead Act and legalize real beer was also introduced. Both were approved by Congress and the amendment was sent to the states for ratification. Butler gave a radio address on the return of real beer in April, and the Ruppert Brewery in Yorkville revved up production and delivered the first barrels to Al Smith, new president of the Empire State Corporation at the Empire State Building.[26]

The 21st Amendment was quickly ratified by the states and became law in December of 1933. New Yorkers, who greeted the Dry Era in 1920 with funereal pomp, celebrated Repeal not only with joy but with a measure of anger after enduring fourteen years of smuggling, bootlegging, raids, and underworld violence. Residents hung an effigy, a caricature of a tall, white male wearing a black suit and top hat and carrying a sign favoring Prohibition, from a flagpole at Broadway and 51st. Others drowned effigies in hotel pools. An American Legion post on Long Island executed an effigy by firing squad.[27]

Congressman La Guardia was elected the city's first Italian/Jewish mayor. He assumed office in January of 1934, vowing to clean up City Hall and naming Lewis J. Valentine his police commissioner. Valentine, insisting that a criminal in police uniform is the worst, fired thousands and rebuked and fined even more. New York gangsters began grumbling among themselves that taking a wagonload of money to City Hall no longer worked. In fact, they said with some surprise, it might even get you arrested.[28]

7

MANAHACTANIENK

While political action was essential to repeal the 18th Amendment, historical forces played a significant role in creating an environment for Repeal, both in New York City and elsewhere. First Amendment rights were powerful, especially the role of freedom of the press in a democracy. Tradition was equally powerful: the political movement for Prohibition was less than a century old, whereas alcohol for enjoyment dates back thousands of years, probably to prerecorded time. Smuggling in American history has a long tradition too, dating to colonial days. Finally, industrialization, immigration, and urbanization in the United States in the late nineteenth and early twentieth centuries created an environment with increasing respect for diversity.

First Amendment Rights

The national media, primarily based in New York City, covered the enforcement and failings of the 18th Amendment more completely than the press covered the wartime debate leading up to ratification. The *New York Times* began reporting violations of the 18th Amendment as early as the fifth month the law was in force. Soon other newspapers were devoting a page a day to violations. The media publicized the exploits of Prohibition agent Izzy Einstein and his partner Moe Smith because the two men provided comic relief with their use of elaborate disguises to get admitted to clubs and speakeasies. Reporters also tended to romanticize smugglers, scofflaws, and sometimes even gangsters. One smuggler told a Manhattan jury that smuggling was not exciting explaining, "That's only newspaper talk."[1]

Representative La Guardia might have remained a lone voice in the dry Congressional wilderness had the media not publicized his point of view beyond Washington. He maintained excellent relationships with the press, and two members of the Wet press unofficially served as his public relations staff. When he decided that the time was ripe for a blatant publicity act in the mid-1920s, he held a press conference in the House Office Building in Washington and another on the sidewalks of Manhattan in front of Leo Kaufman's drugstore at 95 Lenox Avenue. In these two events, he demonstrated any American could produce real beer with two legitimate purchases at a local drugstore—buying a bottle of near beer for ten cents, another of *Leibig's Malt Extract* (3.5 percent alcohol) for 35 cents, and mixing them together. La Guardia invited onlookers, primarily reporters, to try the brew. While the congressman was immune from prosecution in the House Office Building when he made real beer in this fashion, he was liable to arrest in Manhattan and dared a local policeman to arrest him. The cop demurred saying it was a matter for the feds. The media vastly enjoyed covering this event and, back in the pressroom, mixed real beer and declared it delicious before writing their stories. On the other hand, the head of the Prohibition Bureau in Washington mixed a beer, using this method, and pronounced it sufficiently foul-tasting to constitute a violation of the Pure Food and Drug Act. The Bureau then advised druggists not to shelve near beer and malt extract next to each other in their stores. Besides giving La Guardia good publicity, the press portrayed Mayor Walker in a positive light, was amused by John McGill, head of the New York Customs' harbor patrol, and enjoyed the wit of bootleg gangster Vinnie Higgins.

Reporters and editors in Manhattan had a slew of speakeasies and clubs catering to them. The Roxy Grill, at 155 West 46th, was patronized by press agents, theater people, and reporters, and the office building's doorman could smell out federal agents and keep them out. The Press Club, up a flight of stairs at 141 East 46th, was never raided and accessed the best foreign liquor through its members reporting on shipping news at the docks. (When Customs' agents frisked four thousand visitors leaving alcoholic bon voyage parties aboard the docked *Ile de France*, reporters covered the story.) Newsmen and Broadway stars gathered at Billy La Hiff's Tavern on West 48th. There people like Walter Winchell, Gene Fowler, Ed Sullivan, Jack Dempsey, Paul Whiteman, George M. Cohan, Yankees' owner Jacob Ruppert, writers Damon Runyon, Rube Goldberg, Ring Lardner, city editor Stanley Walker, and Mayor Walker exchanged news. John Peron's catered to copy editors for the *New Yorker*. Jack Bleeck's Artist and Writers Club, at 215 West 40th, popular with writers for the *New York Tribune*, was accessed from a door in an adjacent costumes and scenery warehouse used by the Metropolitan Opera. The Dixie Club, in the forties west of Sixth Avenue, had a false front as it if were a cigar store, and was popular with film, theater, and newspaper people.[2]

At the Press Grill, 152 East 41st, reporters from tabloids supposedly concocted stories about smugglers and gangsters, including building up a Bronx hoodlum named Dutch Schultz to boost circulation. Unfortunately, Schultz took this fame to heart and may have escalated his behavior to get more headlines as he was an avid reader, liked seeing his name in print, and reputedly changed his name from Arthur Flegenheimer to Dutch Schultz to fit better in headlines.[3]

Tony's, originally on West 49th Street and then at 59 West 52nd, was run by former Knickerbocker Hotel waiter Tony Soma who started with liquor obtained through his dentist who got it from a longshoreman. Soma's speakeasy was patronized by the media elite, and he kept prices reasonable to attract writers, composers, and theater critics. Vernon Duke first composed "April in Paris" at an old piano at Tony's. Writer Dorothy Parker visited the club late at night accompanied by her dachshund who slept under the table. Harold Ross, the westerner who founded the *New Yorker*, met with writers and editors at Tony's.[4]

The media made midtown night club hostess Mary Louise "Texas" Guinan the best known woman in the entire country. She was on a national list of top celebrities for 1930 along with Henry Ford, Charles Lindbergh, Al Smith, Babe Ruth, and the film dog Rin Tin Tin. Guinan, who began her career as a Texas bronco rider, vaudeville actress, and star in silent Westerns, arrived in Manhattan at the start of Prohibition. She was a charismatic personality in her thirties with long blonde hair, favored big hats, spoke in a loud voice with a Texas twang, and traveled to and from her night clubs in a bulletproof car. There was a constant buzz of excitement whenever she arrived in a club. Patrons relished her irreverent greeting to new arrivals—"Hello Suckers!" Some likened her to a sun queen, a large fireworks display, a circus tamer, or a cowgirl rounding up cattle, the cattle in this case being her customers. Male dancers impersonated her at Manhattan's Roseland Dance Hall, and writer Damon Runyon immortalized her in short stories as "Miss Missouri Martin."[5]

Guinan appeared at many clubs over the years, including Cafe des Beaux Arts, El Fay, Rendezvous, Argonaut, Century, Salon Royal, the Three Hundred, and Club Intime. One of her clubs was simply called the Texas Guinan Club. When one club was padlocked, she moved on to another. She wore a necklace or bracelet with small padlocks in mockery and, if arrested during a raid, would order her orchestra to play the "Prisoner's Song." (When one of her clubs was raided at three in the morning, two U.S. Senators were present as customers.) Her clubs were rumored to have protection from the Broadway Mob, and she successfully avoided jail because she neither owned these clubs nor personally sold any liquor. Rumored to be worth three-quarters of a million dollars by the end of the decade, she would attend St. Patrick's Cathedral on Easter in a Rolls Royce. Guinan died from illness in the final year of Prohibition while visiting the Far West, and her body was returned to Manhattan for the funeral. A crowd of seven thousand stood in the streets watching her hearse while gangsters and bootleggers paid their respects by following the hearse down Broadway in armored cars. Two thousand people came to the cemetery. Orchids and chrysanthemums, in the floral arrangements at the vault, disappeared a few minutes after the graveside service.

Most coverage of Prohibition was in newspapers and magazines, but radio, relatively new and with few listeners at the start of the 1920s, had millions of listeners by the end of the decade. They would tune in to hear Walter Winchell, "King of Broadway," reporting the latest gossip about Manhattan bootleggers and gangsters. People around the country also listened to weekly broadcasts of Duke Ellington's jazz orchestra from the Cotton Club over station WHN.[6]

In 1925, New York publishing houses began producing works about the Prohibition era. The most famous of these was The Great Gatsby by F. Scott Fitzgerald. The novel focused on a New York bootlegger as its main character and also included one minor character named Meyer Wolfsheim, based on Arnold Rothstein. Carl Van Vechten's Nigger Heaven, celebrating Harlem in the 1920s, was published a year after Fitzgerald's novel and received less acclaim. Damon Runyon's contemporary short stories popularized colorful Broadway characters based on

Arnold Rothstein, Larry Fay, detective Johnny Broderick, and hostess
Texas Guinan. (These stories were the basis for the acclaimed Broadway
and Hollywood musical *Guys and Dolls* in the 1950s.) Nonfiction publications in the 1920s, such as *New York Nights* and *That's New York*,
also depicted club and speakeasy life.

When Repeal became a distinct possibility in the early 1930s, New
York publishing houses began producing more nonfiction about the era,
including *The Real McCoy*, *In the Reign of Rothstein*, *Manhattan Oasis*,
and *Night Club Era*. Hollywood also made a contribution in 1931 with
Public Enemy, starring James Cagney who modeled his character after
Manhattan's Owney Madden, even though the film is set in Chicago.
This movie was so popular it ran in a Broadway cinema around the
clock, seven days a week.

Drys got less attention from New York City publishers. U.S. Assistant
Attorney General Mabel Walker Willlebrandt, responsible for enforcing
the Volstead Act, wrote *Inside Prohibition* which was published in "Dry"
Indiana in 1929. The 1932 autobiography of Dry enforcer Izzy Einstein,
entitled *Prohibition Agent No. 1*, had a New York publisher because it
was set in Manhattan and treated Prohibition almost as a comedy.

After Repeal, the press would occasionally revisit Prohibition figures.
This began in the mid-1930s with U.S. Attorney Thomas E. Dewey's
successful prosecution of members of the Broadway Mob, most nota-
bly Charles "Lucky" Luciano and Tammany politician James J. Hines.
Luciano was deported to Italy in the 1940s after finishing his prison
term. Voters rewarded Dewey by electing him governor of New York
State and nominating him as the Republican Party's presidential candidate in 1944 and again in 1948. U.S. Senator Estes Kefauver agreed to
televise his hearings on organized crime in the early 1950s, and Frank
Costello was ordered to appear but refused to be seen on television.
So the camera obligingly focused on his nervous, agitated hands which
were viewed by some thirty million Americans. Lansky did not testify.
(Diamond, Schultz, and Siegel had been executed by the Mob in the
1930s and 40s.) Joe Adonis was deported after those hearings and serious
efforts were made to deport Lansky and Costello, but they hired good
lawyers and were never deported. Costello's case was heard by the U.S.
Supreme Court which eventually concluded that he had not lied on his
citizenship application in the 1920s, by not mentioning his bootlegging
activities which the form did not then require. Lansky sought citizenship in Israel, was asked to leave, and returned to the United States.

Both gangsters died of old age within the United States. Lansky left an estate worth $400 million. Costello's enduring legacy was a famously raspy voice, imitated to great effect by Marlon Brando in Hollywood's first *Godfather* movie which appeared in the last year of Costello's life.[7]

Respect for Tradition

Mayor Walker claimed that New York City in his time had more Irishmen (400,000) than Dublin, more Italians (800,000) than Rome, more Germans (500,000) than any city except Berlin, and more Jews (more than a million) than Palestine. Liquor was central to these cultures more than a thousand years before ratification of the 18th Amendment in the United States. St. Patrick, patron saint of Ireland, supposedly introduced whiskey to the Irish. In ancient Rome the popular saying, "In vino veritas" recognized that human beings were more likely to speak the truth under the influence of wine. The Germans brewed beer in the fourth century or earlier. And Jesus of Nazareth's first miracle was turning water into wine at a Jewish wedding.[8]

Early American history also records the centrality of liquor. The Pilgrims reputedly stopped in New England partly because their beer supply on board ship was exhausted. Immigrants to colonial Virginia were told to bring their own malt supply until they could build up immunity to the local water. Young Patrick Henry tended bar in his uncle's tavern. George Washington brewed beer at Mount Vernon. Paul Revere fortified himself with rum before riding out to warn colonists the British were coming. And John Marshall, fourth and most famous Chief Justice of the U.S. Supreme Court, was known to be so fond of quality Madeira that citizens began calling it "Supreme Court."[9]

The first rebellion under the U.S. Constitution was over liquor, taxes, and the national debt. Scots-Irish farmers in western Pennsylvania converted leftover grain and corn to whiskey for easier transport over the mountains to Eastern markets and for local use as a medium of exchange. When Congress passed an excise tax on whiskey to reduce the national debt, the frontiersmen in western Pennsylvania threatened to rebel. President Washington assembled an army, marched in their direction, and they quickly disbursed, thus ending the Whiskey Rebellion of 1794.

Smuggling has also been part of the American tradition. Before the Revolution, British Navigation Acts placed import duties on molasses not transported directly from England or carried in British ships. This was to discourage U.S. colonists from trading directly for molasses and rum with the French West Indies. Boston merchant John Hancock smuggled rum and became as famous in American history for that feat as for signing the Declaration of Independence in large script so King George III could easily read the Hancock name.[10]

Smuggling in defiance of the federal government was also in the historical tradition. Despite a clause in the Constitution providing for an end to the international slave trade after 1808 and Congressional approval for such a ban, African slaves were smuggled into the South up to the Civil War. Ten years before the Civil War, a pro-slavery Congress passed a Fugitive Slave Act making it illegal to smuggle slaves North to freedom, yet abolitionists smuggled them anyway via the famous Underground Railroad.

Captain Bill McCoy, Prohibition's most famous smuggler, knew this American history and claimed he was in the tradition of Hancock, slave smugglers, and abolitionists.

Respect for Diversity

The Dry movement took root in a primarily rural, agricultural nation in the 1800s still dominated by white Anglo-Saxon Protestants (WASPs). Alcohol was popular when the only other drinks easily available were coffee, tea, raw milk, and water. (Canned soda, a popular modern drink, did not exist.) As a result, alcoholism was a major social problem. The proposed Prohibition amendment was viewed as a viable solution.

At the same time, industrialization was beginning to contribute to a demographic shift away from the family farm to factories and cities. This shift accelerated as millions of immigrants settled in cities, particularly New York City. For the first time, in 1930, more than half the population of the United States lived in urban areas. This simple fact was of great significance in explaining the success of Repeal.

The New Yorker magazine, founded in Manhattan in the midst of Prohibition, was indicative of this demographic shift. Drys had always considered cities as necessary evils. But now more and more Americans understood cities to be the wave of the future. This change in attitude toward cities is reflected in the fact that a significant portion of early subscribers to the New Yorker were urban Americans living elsewhere in the country. The Empire State Building, completed the same year as Repeal (1933), was an even more visible symbol than the *New Yorker* of the rise of New York City in public esteem. That structure was not only the tallest in the nation but, at the time, the tallest in the world.[11]

In addition to their failure to assess the importance of cities in the nation's future, Drys failed to appreciate the lasting power of Manhattan's unique past. In the early seventeenth century, New Amsterdam was a trading center positioned on two rivers with easy access to the ocean and, hence, the North American coast. Sixteen languages were spoken in New Amsterdam. Liquor was central to its colonial culture. Its first burgomaster was a brewer. Its first brewery in an area near Wall Street. Its first European-American baby (a girl) grew up to become a brewer. Native Americans coined a word to describe the early settlement of these Europeans. That word was *Manahactanienk* or "place of general inebriation."

Little wonder then that New York City, hundreds of years later, would live up to this earlier reputation. During Prohibition, its smugglers, bootleggers, and scofflaws were an effective, informal resistance movement contributing significantly to the demise of the unpopular 18th Amendement.[12]

Appendix

SELECTED PRIMARY DOCUMENTS

Ten letters from the
National Archives Prohibition Collections

1. Agnes McCardle to Assistant U.S. Attorney General Mabel Walker Willebrandt, 1924.

On or about Nov. 16, the rum-running tug *William P. Maloney* was lost with a cargo of liquor and with her 12 men. We have reason to believe we had a brother on board. On going to the owner's home, Captain [John] McCambridge of 159 Kent Street, Brooklyn, New York, we were denied all information and they denied ownership of the boat. However, records in the New York Custom House show her to be owned by a man named Aaron who, we later discovered, is employed by this McCambridge in the capacity of selling liquor for him. This man is also called "Murphy" by his associates. Captain McCambridge has an office at Pier 38's Atlantic Dock under the name of White Band Towing Line.

This is the second boat lost by this man, as records will show, the other one went down with 16 men aboard and a cargo of liquor about two years ago. That boat was in the name of Margaret Kinman, his sister. This man boasts of his pull and also about his knowledge of the rum scandal in Jersey of which he knows plenty because he had bought liquor right there. This man is living in luxury while the families of the men are in want and [he] is still active in the rum business.

The name of the boat he lost two years ago was the *Lizzie D*. His boats are not fit for sailing purposes. Please give this your attention and save this sorrow. This man is a menace to the business of men who work on boats. Enclosed [news]clippings can tell you more than I.

2. Anonymous letter to Department of Justice, Washington, D.C. September 1930.

The *Paul Jones*, trawler with $30,000 cargo, just caught by the Coast Guard off Jones Inlet belonged to the Frankel-Barbarie-Grossman syndicate of rum runners in Long Beach. The boat fired on off Baldwin about a month ago was also one of this syndicate.

Long Beach police stand guard along the ocean while boats are unloaded between 3 and 4 o'clock in the morning. Anyone passing [by] is not allowed within a block of the ocean by the motorcycle police. County police are also taken care of.

Only Department of Justice men, with the help of the Coast Guard, can break this up. Check telephone calls to Grossman. Too much money being divided locally for any results.

3. George W. Ellison to the U.S. Treasury Department, Washington D.C., [January? 1930]

I have advised both Captain Wolff of the New London Coast Guard base and also [Prohibition Bureau] undercover agents O'Keefe and Milk in New York that the responsible persons in the Long Island liquor ring responsible for the *Flor del Mar* rum ship captured several weeks ago was operated by Budd King of East Hampton, Long Island, and Emerson Tabor of the same town.

These men have been landing liquor cargoes each month, between seven and ten thousand cases, aided by one Turnbull who was once connected with the Coast Guard base of New London and who, by the way, has been receiving inside information from the base at New London.

Operations are from an outside boat via radio to smaller vessels who leave the base at Montauk Point and go east to Block Island or west to Shinnecock Lightship, meet, take their cargo, keep in constant touch with two small boats that are operated by King, also with wireless sets, who keep on the lookout for government patrol boats in the vicinity of Fort Pond, Promised Land, and Gardners Bay, giving you an illustration. [hand-drawn map included]. King operates radio lookout boats advising loading boats what place to use for unloading, also sending them out to sea if it happens to be dangerous. After once landing, it becomes very easy for all the police in East and South Hampton to receive a monthly allowance for allowing the trucks to proceed to New York.

You may also advise the Internal Revenue collectors that King and Emerson keep their money made this way in the savings vault of the East Hampton bank. Trusting this information is of some use to you.

4. Anonymous letter from New Jersey resident to Brig. General Lincoln C. Andrews, director of a new division in the U.S. Treasury which combined agents from the Prohibition Bureau, Customs, and the Coast Guard, c. 1925.

Herewith is a tip which will make your work easy in regards to rum getting ashore at Sea Bright, N.J. There is a man called Rubie Wilbur at [Coast Guard?] 99 Station and other men there who hang out at Charlie Rogers on Church Street, Sea Bright. Another man is a captain now. Watch him—Joe Tilton. These men capture cargo at sea. This Charlie Rogers goes to sea and gets a load from the guards and sells it for these men on commission: he always has rum stored at his house. This Wilbur got his forty cases about a month ago when the *Lynx II* came ashore at Sandy Hook and Charlie, or "Mickey" Rogers, sold it on commission for him. They always hang round there. You got the right dope now—a ship to guard a ship at Rum Row.

Mantolokin, New Jersey, is another place runners could buy protection. This Harold Bitters, shot recently, is the one you have to buy a ticket from for rum when you go to sea. He's from the Highlands. Mr. Andrews, the guards here never take a boat or a man landing [the liquor]; they only want the rum.

Charlie Rogers hides his under his house. His son worked awhile at the 99 Station as a sub. Good luck to you and I guess some of these Coast Guards[men] won't be getting any more closed cars. Tilton had a good record, but he's slick, he works with "Mickey." I'm with you

Mr. Andrews, but I do not want to be known. Captain Butter at the [Sandy] Hook is a square man but he ain't got the nerve to get 'em. This is a red hot tip, Mr. Andrews, and if you act you'll get the goods at Roger's [house]. If you don't find it in his house, dig in sand under his house.

I am not signing who I am for I'm afraid it may be known, but I'm with you and I never ran rum or drank it, and I'm glad there is someone to write to who has no ropes on him.

5. Anonymous letter from Fulton Fish Market Visitor, December 1924.

On December 12, I was in New York and was looking around the waterfront. I called at the fish market at Fulton Street, New York City, and went on board the yacht *Madeline D.* owned in Halifax, Nova Scotia, and managed by a New York rum Christmas trade. I reported it to the Coast Guard Station at South Ferry, New York City, and was to see the Customs Collector, Mr. Hamilton [too], but being Saturday and noon, could not see him so I came on to Lynn [Massachusetts.]

Five men came down to the *Madeline D.* and started the engine to try it out and stayed until 5 p.m. when the [Massachusetts] *Bay State Line Passenger Boat* left and I was a passenger on board. Before leaving, I went and put the number of the car, license 84.289, to the man from the Department at New York. And they can get the owner of the car and the rum ring on board. The cook on the boat is an American citizen named Jame Delane Priest. Priest is a nickname. At Gloucester, Massachusetts, he is known as Jimmy DePriest. The captain is a Newfoundlander. The mate is also from the same place but lives in Brooklyn, New York The remainder of the crew is from Newfoundland. I could not find out who the supercargo was. There are seven men on board fitted out with one month's food and water. No fishing hoses. Only two chains as they intend laying by instead of at anchor.

I told them [authorities] in New York to send a plainclothes man down to look her [*Madeline D.*] over. You might ask them just what they found out. Now I am not getting anything for my work in helping to stop the rum running, but I feel it is my duty to do so. And anything I can do I will do to enforce the law. So please let them know in New York, Mr. Hamilton at Customs House, and also the Coast Guard at the South Ferry Station, New York, N.Y.

6. Coast Guard Telegram to shore, 1925, concerning a fishing boat headed for Fulton Fish Market.

THE SCHOONER [Annie Louise] HAS FISHING LICENSE. HER DESTINATION DID NOT APPEAR ON PAPERS. CAPTAIN SAYS THAT NEW YORK MARKET IS BEST. HAS CARGO FROM THREE OTHER FISHING SCHOONERS THAT ARE ON THE [Fishing] GROUNDS. SHE HAS A CARGO OF COD FISH. DO NOT KNOW WHOM CONSIGNEE IS.

AM STILL STANDING BY SCHOONER. SHE IS STILL HEADED FOR NEW YORK. IF SHE HAS CONTRABAND, IT IS BENEATH HER CARGO. DID NOT MOVE CARGO AS I AM SHORT-HANDED. SUGGEST SHE BE WATCHED WHEN UNLOADED. REQUEST INSTRUCTIONS.

7. Letter of New York Coast Guard Division Commander A. J. Henderson to Commander Charles S. Root, Washington D.C., 17 May 1927.

Fulton Market is in New York City, only a comparatively short distance up the East River from the Battery. I have endeavored for months past to impress upon the Customs authorities here the necessity for supervising the unloading of all fish cargoes arriving at Fulton Market. On numerous occasions, patrol boats have followed fishing vessels from the Narrows to Fulton Market where they were supposed to be taken over by Customs inspectors. In many instances I was afterwards notified that no liquor was landed from these vessels and that a final inspection of them after the fish had been unloaded showed that there had been no liquor on board. All the same I have believed that these fishermen were bringing in liquor. In my opinion reliable inspectors should be at Fulton Market at all times and a rigid inspection should be made of the unloading of all fish cargoes. It has been reported in the past that crates of fish have been unloaded and placed on trucks and that they contained liquor with a covering of fish on top. . . .

8. Statement of Fred Christopherson, crewman aboard S.S. Corsica, 31 August, 1925.

I, Fred Christopherson, make the following statement of my own free will and accord and after being advised of my constitutional rights, knowing that this statement may be used for or against me, and it is made without promise or threats.

I am 45 years of age, born at Marinette, Wisconsin, and had been on the *Corsica* for two years as a fireman, when the ship was chartered for the trip to Bath, Maine, with cargo of coal and my wages were $76.50 per month. The vessel left Newport News, Virginia, for Bath, Maine, July 22 1925, at which place the coal was discharged, and we sailed July 30th and went to sea. After we were out on the sea for about 24 hours, I was informed that we were to meet a ship and take on a cargo of rum, but did not find the ship and returned to Boston and took on bunker coal and supplies. None of the crew was allowed shore leave while in Boston except Captain Baker, owner Reaves, and two members of the rum gang. We left Boston after securing supplies and put to sea, cruising around off the Nova Scotia coast, when early on the morning of August 9th we sighted the rum boat, a three masted schooner, name unknown, from which we secured about 4000 cases of various liquors.

We then proceeded to Long Island by way of the East River, arriving at Oyster Bay where we unloaded a part of the cargo only as it became daylight. We then went to what I thought was off Huntington Cove where we anchored for the day. That evening we went back to where we were the night before and finished unloading the cargo. Then we left for Newport News by way of Montauk Point. . . .

While we were [first] going out to sea to meet the rum ship, Captain Baker came around among the crew and told us we would each receive a bonus of $100 if we made a successful trip. I did not receive the bonus and as yet have not received my wages. While out on the rum expedition, there were several of the rum crew carrying guns, especially one who was demonstrating his marksmanship by shooting at things drifting by, the bullets plainly being heard by the crew. While they did not openly threaten us, it tended to intimidate those members of the crew who did not belong to the rum gang.

9. Letters of James Regno, alias Jimmie Allen, New York liquor dealer in Havana, 1927 to friend Irene in New York City.

Received two letters from you which sure was a pleasure, to hear from you and that your mother and boy and your sister were asking for me. I haven't much to say because everything looks Bad except that Charlie

[Levy] and I are still waiting for those two boats by Miles and Guins. I received a cable from Miles a week ago today to wire him three hundred dollars for repairs for the yacht [*Winona*], which I did. And haven't heard anything from them yet but will wait until Monday or Tuesday. If they don't come or wire me by then, I will leave for New York and be back by Thursday or Friday. But if things will change by then, I will write and let you know about it. . . . Well as to say anything about Charlie and myself, we are very much disappointed on the deal. They have either double-crossed us or done something wrong. Otherwise I am feeling fine and in the best of health. Well as to anything about myself and Charlie,we are very blue, but more so myself. I am losing some money and nothing to show, but there is no use of worry if I come back. I will get my boat and come right back here. For there is plenty of work here.

Well, I hope this letter reaches you before I get home as it leaves me in the very best of health. I will close with love to you.

10. Letter of Father A. Romano to sons Captain Michaelangelo Romano and Antonio Romano, 1924. [Romano's ship was seized in Huntington Bay.]

My adored sons: Today I received another letter from you in which you tell me of the charter. Frankly, I tell you, if in time, I would advise against it, for this is another kind of contraband [first was illegal immigrants] in which the revenue is defrauded, and then Venza, being mixed up in it, it will be a repetition of the first. Be careful of the vessel. Don't let them eat it up on you. That is the object which Venza and someone else aim at. Make them pay you the chartering in anticipation and if you have any trouble make them pay before the discharge of the merchandise. This is a business in which you cannot make any [legal] claims afterwards.

Congressional Testimony of U.S. Attorney Emory Buckner to Senate Judiciary Subcommittee, 7 April 1926.
[U.S. Senate, 69th U.S. Congress, Proceedings of the Judiciary Subcommittee on the National Prohibition Law.]

My name is Emory R. Buckner. I reside at 30 East 67th Street, New York City [Silk Stocking District.] I am United States Attorney for the

Southern District of New York and am here in response to a subpoena
sent me by the Sergeant at Arms of the United States Senate. My district includes the county of Manhattan, the county of the Bronx, the
county of Westchester, and the eight contiguous counties running to a
point just south of Albany, 11 counties in all. I regret to say that I do
not know the population of my district, but I assume it is somewhere
between 6,000,000 and 8,000,000 people. . . .

Not only in my study of the prohibition question in my district in
New York City, but from talking with a very large number of people
who have discussed with me the prohibition question and who come
from other parts of the country, I reach the conclusion that the fun-
damental misconception of national prohibition is as follows: I regard
the national prohibition law as a declaration of war against the liquor
traffic. But it seems to me that altogether too many people regard it
as a treaty of peace, in which a part of the country agreed to buy no
more liquor, and a part of the country agreed to sell no more liquor,
and then the war was over. . . .

I am repeatedly asked, and I presume I would have been asked by
this committee, whether in my judgment the prohibition law could be
enforced in my district. My reply to that question has to be that I do
not know, because in my judgement as a prosecutor the prohibition law,
by which I mean the Volstead law or cognate State laws, which we did
have for a time [Mullan Gage Enforcement Act in New York State]
has never been tried in New York City in a way which would make
enforcement effective. It has never been tried by the Federal Government in my judgment in my district, not only during my term of office
but before my term of office. . . .

Before assuming office in March 1925, I spent nearly a month making a survey in the Federal building. I found that a very large number
of people were being brought into the Federal building for violation
of the Volstead law. I found that a great majority of these defendants
were being brought in by members of the New York City police department. It is difficult to estimate, but after talking with the United States
commissioner and other officials during my survey, I think it is not far
wrong to say that close to 50,000 violators of the Volstead laws were
being brought into the Federal building in the course of a year, by both
the city police and the prohibition agents. I, myself, went up to the
Federal building and spent many days there. I found one United States
commissioner without a stenographer because none is provided, without

court attendants because none are provided. I found the fifth floor of the Federal building a seething mob of bartenders, peddlers, waiters, bond runners, fixers. . . .

Federal judges have told me that the whole atmosphere of the Federal building was one of pollution, that the air of corruption had even descended into the civil parts of the court, and reports were made to the senior United States judge of attempts to bribe jurymen even in the toilets of the building. . . . between $200,00 and $300,000 of bonds had been forfeited and yet the bonding companies had not paid up. . . . 99 per cent or more of the people arrested were not the men who were making money but the subordinates, the employees. . . . I found that prohibition agents were being promoted, or were being rated, by the number of arrests they made, not the number of convictions, not the quality of arrests, not the amount of liquor stopped. . . .

I found that the police commissioner of the city of New York when I took office was receiving 15,000 complaints a month or 180,000 a year of violations of the Volstead law in the city, almost wholly speakeasy complaints or saloon complaints. They were complaints from neighbors and citizens made to the police commissioner. And he told me that he should be removed from office if he did not attempt to do something in that situation even without any help in the State courts. . . .

[Question by Senator]. I wish you would recite what the part of the foreign element that you have in that big city might be in the matter of the prosecutions for criminal violations?

[Buckner.] Do you mean as to whether or not the foreign elements are in bootlegging rather than——

[Senator.] Yes.

[Buckner.] As bootlegger, supply man or consumer?

[Senator.] Either.

[Buckner.] Well, I do not know Senator. It is certainly not so marked that it has become a matter of such comment that it has reached me yet. . . . . . .

[Another Senator.] Do you find juries in New York City fairly responsive to the facts as developed?

[Buckner.] We have only tried on the strictly criminal angle some thirty odd cases . . . all within the last six months . . . and we have secured convictions by picking out the men higher up, and important people, we have secured jail sentences after trial of about 15 years, the aggregate. . . . And we have received pleas of guilty in still cases, manufacturing cases, where the defendants felt that we could convict them and get a jail sentence. I have been wholly unable to wheedle a jail settlement out of a man who is only arrested for selling. . . . a feeling on the part of New York, New York being what it is, that the prohibition law you cannot work up as much of excitement on the prohibition law as you can work up on a commercial fraud case. And I think that great injustice has been done prohibition enforcement by assuming that New York juries won't convict. We prosecuted Steinberg, a millionaire bootlegger, for defrauding in his income tax after he had been acquitted some two or three years before in a prohibition case. . . .

[Buckner on drugstores] There are in our district 17 [federal] agents whose duty is to examine 12,000 drugstores and check up on 5000 physicians. Therefore the business which we find has been bootlegged, the business which they are expected to stop, amounts to practically one million dollars per man . . . But I would want more than a $2000 man [annual salary of federal agent] to be responsible for stopping a business of one million dollars a year. . . . . .

[Buckner asked about smuggling.] Within the last four weeks we have picked up two boats, one made by the [Marine] police department entirely, simply tugs that came in from Rum Row, and the other I believe by police and Customs in collaboration. Both seizures were made on an anonymous tip telephoned to me . . . and it is my opinion that there is much less smuggling of liquor since the Coast Guard had been rendered more efficient than there was before [1924].

[Senator.] Do you think the seizures and confiscations have made the [smuggling] business so unprofitable that it has been abandoned to some extent?

Buckner: I do not know.

Selected Passages from Congressional Speeches of
Fiorello La Guardia, 1925–30.

February 7, 1925, 68th Congress, second session.
[La Guardia's reaction on being told that New York was one of the wet
spots in the United States.]

Well if you stop to consider how many transients we have in New
York every day coming from the real dry districts, I can readily understand how there is a great demand for liquor in the city. . . .

[He supports appropriations and measures to enforce prohibition as
long as it is the law.] But at the end of a ten year period from the time
of enactment of the Volstead Act, I am going to ask for a hearing on
the floor of the House, and then we ought to take an inventory and
see whether or not this law is capable of enforcement.

May 1, 1929.
I charge that the Federal government, vested with the duty and respon-
sibilities of law enforcement throughout the United States, is making no
attempt to enforce the prohibition law equally throughout the United
States. . . . enforcement is being concentrated in a few large centers.
Here is the proof: the Bureau of Prohibition of the Treasury Department
has assigned to the State of New York, with an area of 47,654 square
miles and a population of 11,550,000, 338 prohibition agents, inspectors,
and investigators while the States of Virginia, North Carolina, South
Carolina, Florida, Georgia, Louisiana, Mississippi, Alabama, Kentucky,
Tennessee, and Puerto Rico, with an area of 461,436 square miles and
a population of 24,818,600, ten times the area of New York State,
two and one-half times the population of New York, but 297 agents
and investigators are enforcing prohibition. . . . centering the bulk of
the 1,872 prohibition enforcement officials in New York City, Chicago,
Philadelphia, St. Louis, San Francisco. The Government, by its very
attitude, says that the law shall be enforced in isolated spots and there
be no enforcement to speak of anywhere else. . . .

January 7, 1930.
Let us look at these cold facts as they exist. Let us not differ on questions of established facts. Then taking the facts as they are, let us face
the problem courageously. That is the duty of the American Congress.
If prohibition is not creating a temperate, abstaining people, then it

is not a success. Men and women who are sincerely interested in the cause of temperance, and desirous of bringing about total abstinence must be convinced that prohibition will not do it. Other countries have tried. Norway, Denmark, Sweden, Finland, Belgium, and Canada have all tried prohibition. Norway, Denmark, and Canada went though the same conditions we are now experiencing. All these countries, with one exception, were compelled to modify their prohibition laws and to place the traffic under proper regulation and supervision. The change brought temperance and the consumption of liquor is less now than when they had complete prohibition. . . . There is more drinking going on per capita in Finland than any other country in Europe. Finland and the United States are now the only two countries struggling with bone-dry prohibition. . . . We must face the situation and do the next thing, admit its failure and so change the law so as to meet the views and desires, habits, and customs of a vast majority of the people of this country.

NOTES

Author's Note

1. United States National Archives and Records Administration [NARA], Record Group 26, Coast Guard Seized Vessels 1920–33, *Clackamas* file. R.G. 26 consists of 90 archival boxes of files, organized alphabetically by name of the vessel. These records were confidential until the 1990s.

2. For etymology of scofflaw, see *New York Times*, 10.11.1952.

3. See Malcolm Willoughby, *Rum War at Sea* (Washington, DC: Government Printing Office, 1964) and Michael Lerner, *Dry Manhattan* (Cambridge, MA: Harvard University Press, 2007). These two histories provided good overviews as well as significant details on smuggling, in the first case, and on speakeasies, clubs, and political figures in the second.

4. See Mábel W. Willebrandt, *Inside Prohibition* (Indianapolis, IN: Bobbs-Merrill, 1929) for "Babylon-on-the-Hudson" term, page 99. The *Satan* term appears in Lerner, *Dry Manhattan*.

Preface

1. Besides Willoughby's *Rum Wars* and Lerner's *Dry Manhattan*, these general histories of Prohibition were helpful: Frederick Lewis Allen, *Only Yesterday* (New York: Harper & Row, 1931); Kenneth Allsop, *Bootleggers and Their Era* (New York: Doubleday, 1961); Herbert Asbury, *The Great Illusion: An Informal History of Prohibition* (Westport, CT: Greenwood Press, 1968 reprint); Edward Behr, *Thirteen Years that Changed America* (New York: Arcade, 1996); Isadore Einstein, *Prohibition Agent No. 1* (New York: Frederick Stokes, 1932); Henry Lee, *How Dry We Were* (Englewood Cliffs, NJ: Prentice Hall, 1963); and Stan-

ley Walker, Night Club Era (New York: Frederick Stokes Co., 1933). During Prohibition it remained legal to make liquor for export when authorized by the government. The National Distilleries Products Corporation, with one-third of all legal, bonded spirits in the nation, owned the Kentucky Distilleries and Warehouse Company headquartered in Manhattan. (See *Wickersham Commission Report*, v. 4, #5.)

Chapter 1. Rum Row

1. In January 1920, the Green River Distilling Company's barge, loaded with liquor for storage in the British West Indies, sank amidst ice floes in the Hudson River near West 94.

2. NARA, R.G. 26, Entry 179A-1, *Mazel Tov*.

3. Op. Cit., *Henry Marshall, Arethusa/Tomoka*. See also Frederick Van de Water, *The Real McCoy* (New York: Doubleday, 1931).

4. See mention of *Fidus* in Willoughby, *Rum Wars*, 31 and 35, and see NARA, R.G. 26 for *John W. Dwight*, especially 8.28.1925 report on the sinking that occurred 4.5.1923. New Yorkers Thomas Craven, Captains King and Carmichael, John J. Ryan, and Edward Snyder had financial interests in the *Dwight*.

5. Van de Water, *McCoy*, 274. According to McCoy, Eddie was thrown overboard from the last returning pirate ship.

6. NARA, R.G. 26, *Mulhouse* and Willoughby, *Rum Wars*, 54. Possible pirate boats from New York and Nova Scotia were: *Patara; Catherine Marie of Nassau; Clark Corkum; Maud Thornhill; M. M. Gardiner; Mary Conrad; Tessia Aubrey; Quaco Queen;* and *Genevieve*.

7. NARA, R.G. 26, *Veronica, Nancy*. See Willoughby, *Rum Wars*, 36–38, for the cases of *Patricia M. Berman* and *Yankton*.

8. See Van de Water, *McCoy*, 240, and Asbury, *Great Illusions*, for mention of garbage scows and Willoughby, *Rum Wars*, 65. See also NARA, R.G. 26, *Brooklyn* (sewage barge) and *Josephine*.

9. See Van de Water, *McCoy*, and Willoughby, *Rum Wars*, 33 and 91, for ships wrecked in storms off Sandy Hook (*Jennie Bell*) and Montauk (*Madonna V*).

10. NARA, R.G. 26, *William Maloney, Dorothy, Lizze D. Henrietta*. New Yorkers who went down with the *Maloney* were: Captain Roscoe Jenkins, 110 Lexington Avenue, Manhattan, former policeman; Charles Cox, Frances Goodman; Joseph Murphy; Timothy Coofey; Frederick Holt; Patrick Donovan; Joseph Freeman; Thomas Drudy; Walter O'Hagen; Robert Bondes; and John Olson. McCambridge, the ship's owner, lived in Brooklyn, and worked in office of the White Band Towing Line on Pier 38's Atlantic Dock.

11. NARA, R.G. 25, *Dick, Butterfly*.

12. See George Wolf with Joseph DiMorra, *Frank Costello: Prime Minister of the Underworld* (New York: William Morrow, 1974).

13. NARA, R.G. 26, *Pictonian, Over the Top, Sagatind.* Willoughby, *Rum Wars*, 53–54, maintains that the Norwegian crew was continually drunk and fought among themselves, and does not mention this as a test case, nor that reparations were eventually made by the U.S. Congress.

14. NARA, R.G. 26, *Underwriter* and *Ruth Mildred.*

15. Willoughby, *Rum Wars*, 164.

16. NARA, R.G. 26, *W.H. Eastwood and Sangucenti.*

17. NARA, R.G. 26, *Beatrice* and *Rask.*

18. NARA, R.G. 26, *Madeline E. Adams* and *Gaspe Fisherman.* The Coast Guard believed the *Mazel Tov*, found 11.5 miles south of Martha's Vineyard, was illegally there and seized it. Later the courts determined that particular ship could go no faster than 10 mph and, according to the "one hour" term in the treaty, was within its legal rights half a mile in from the usual 12-mile limit.

19. NARA, R.G. 26, *T.A.D. Jones* and Willoughby, *Rum Wars*, 133–134.

20. Ibid., *Dorothy M. Smart, Mary, James B.*

21. See Willoughby, *Rum Wars*, 105–113, entry on Ms. Friedman in *Wikipedia*, and Mabel W. Willebrandt, *Inside Prohibition*, 234. For radio see also NARA, R.G. 10 National Commission on Prohibition, Boxes 206–207 and R.G. 26 for *Gray Phantom, Beatrice L., Alma R., Newton Bay, Nova V,* and *Winnie.*

22. NARA, R.G. 26, *Maurice Tracy.*

23. See Van de Water, *McCoy*, on pilot buzzing the Coast Guard, Willoughby, *Rum Wars*, 51 and 108, and NARA, R.G. 26, *Gray Phantom.*

24. NARA, R.G. 26, *Lommergain.* [Note Willoughy, *Rum Wars*, only mentions one Coast Guard plane, borrowed, and includes no index entry for planes or airplanes.]

25. NARA, R.G. 26, 178-A, intelligence folder on submarines. See also *Washington Post*, 6.30.1924 and 8.3.24, *New York Times*, 8.3.1924, *New York Herald Tribune*, 8.3.1924, and Wolf, *Costello*, 61.

26. NARA, R.G. 26, *Rose of Marlboro, Arco Felice II, Winona, Edward Westerdeke.* See also *Fred B.*

27. See Van de Water, *McCoy*, 198, John P. King, *Wicked Tales from the Highlands* (ebook, 2011), 56, and Willoughby, *Rum Wars*, 154.

28. See Gertrude Lythgoe, *Bahama Queen: An Autobiography* (New York: Exposition Press, 1964).

29. See Van de Water, *McCoy*, 175, and NARA, R.G. 26, *Wydabiity, Mary E. Diebold,* and *Ekers.*

Chapter 2. Along the Shore

1. NARA, R.G. 26, *Algie, Flor del Mar, Mistinguette, Sumatra, Sylvester, Zip.* The *Mistinguette* was seized off Amagansett and *Sumter* tossed liquor overboard off Montauk Point Lightship.

2. Ibid., *Surf, Hattie T.* See also Nicole Flotteron, "Rum Running, Boot-legging, and Pirates on the East End of Long Island," www.hamptons.com/Home-and-Garden, and Willoughby, *Rum Wars*, 101.

3. NARA, R.G. 26, *Magdalene, Sylvester, Temiscouda,* and Flotteron, "Rum Running." Seymour Hersh, *The Dark Side of Camelot* (Boston: Little, Brown, 1997), 48, claimed liquor consigned to Joseph Kennedy, father of the future president, was delivered to a cove in Sag Harbor, Long Island, during Prohibition.

4. Ibid., *Notus* for both quotes.

5. Ibid., *Del Ray II, Helen G. McLean, Pinta, Patricia. Roamer of Montauk* seized in fog on Napeague Bay.

6. Ibid., *Commodore, Nova V, Desiree, Alice Jane.*

7. Ibid., *Maud S. II, S.F. Burns.*

8. Ibid., *Edward Westerdeke.* The crew of *Winifred H.* fled to Bay Shore after the ship was seized.

9. Ibid., *Zeehond, J.B. Young,* and NARA, Dept. of Treasury, Entry 191, R.G. 56, *Albertina.*

10. *New York Times*, 9.3.1922. See also NARA, R.G. 26, for *Vince, Mary Mother Elizabeth,* and *U.S. vs. Wylk and Blohm*, 6.2.1930.

11. NARA. R.G. 26, *Mary Mother Elizabeth, Three Links, William H. Landry, Henrietta, Vince,* and *Dorothy M. Smart* were ships in the Wylk gang.

12. Ibid., *San Jose, William H. Albury.*

13. Ibid., *Paul Jones* for correspondence to Dept. of Justice, September 1930.

14. Ibid., *Warbug, Fantasma, Consuelo,* and *Virginia,* the latter seized off Orient Point, Long Island. See also Willoughby, *Rum Wars*, 94.

15. Ibid., *Flor del Mar, Cote Nord,* and T. Levy, "Days of Rum Running, *Shoreline [Ct.] Times* 11.12.2011.

16. NARA, R.G. 26, *George Cochran, William A. Morse, Stroller.*

17. Ibid., *Arco Felice II, Yita R.* Captain Romano also handled the *Dori* (*Zetti*), which illegally attempted to land 130 to 170 Sicilian men near New York City but was foiled by the Coast Guard. He then landed them in Nova Scotia and most were caught and deported.

18. Ibid., *Arco Felice II* and *Viola.* Willoughby, *Rum Wars*, 96–97, mentions the Italian ship but not that the case involving it was eventually reversed. *Viola* was abandoned on Eaton's Neck near Huntington Bay.

19. NARA, R.G. 26, *Corsica, W.T. Bell,* and *New York Herald Tribune* 1.7.1924. In the early 1920s, Frank Costello killed or ordered killed a smuggler, named Louie De Mar of Baysville, for double-crossing him according to Leonard Katz, *Uncle Frank: The Biography of Frank Costello* (New York: Drake, 1973), 59.

20. Ibid., *France, Idle Hour.* The *Pocomoke* was seized off Black Point, Connecticut. Allen, *Only Yesterday*, 246, mentions Rhode Island and Connecticut were the only two holdouts on ratification of the 18th Amendment.

21. Ibid., *Scipio*.

22. Ibid., *William H. Moody, Storm Petrell, Donetta*.

23. Ibid., *Tertia*.

24. Ibid., *Harbour Trader, Caucasier, Wanderlust, Mayflower*. See Willoughby, *Rum Wars*, 107 on radios.

25. NARA, R.G. 26, *Oblay, Mary of New Bedford*.

26. Willoughby, *Rum Wars*, 32 and 103. NARA, R.G. 26, *Java, Woodgod, Saint Pierraise, Maurice Tracy*. The *Woodgod* was seized in Jamaica Bay.

27. See Carl Sifakis, *Mafia Encyclopedia* (New York: Checkmark, 1999) for background, and King, *Wicked Tales from the Highlands*, 46–50. See Allsop, *Bootleggers*, 298, for information that the Harvard Inn was a liquor drop during Prohibition.

28. NARA, R.G. 26, *Syzygy, Whatzis*. McCambridge owned *William Maloney, Lorraine Rita, Timothy*. Stack owned *Vereign*, and Entenza owned *Fantasma*.

29. NARA, R.G. 26, *Nova V.* and 178-A, -1, Box 20, radio files, and Willoughby, *Rum Wars*, 172.

30. Ibid., *Albatross, Storm Petrell, Gaspe Fisherman, Thorndyke* were Fox ships.

31. Ibid., *Toxaway, Standard Coaster, Service*.

32. Lee, *How Dry*, 120–122 on Hammerstein "Mansion." According to Lee, the body of a murdered Newark bootlegger, Al Lillien, was found neatly laid out on the top floor of the "Estate" and gray gloves were found on a table in the library along with two revolvers and two decks of cards, both topped by a King of Spades face up. King, *Wicked Tales*, 51, and NARA, R.G. 26, S.C. 217 and *Mercury*. Captain McCoy's first boat, the slow-moving *Marshall*, was seized off Sea Bright.

33. NARA, R.G. 26, *Charmain II, Jean-Louis*. See Willoughby, *Rum Wars*, 35, on *P.J. McLaughlin*.

34. King, *Wicked Tales*, 46. See NARA, R.G. 26, *Maud Thornhill* and *Margaret Witte*.

35. NARA, R.G. 26, *Atalanta, Julito*. See also Willoughby, *Rum Wars*, 69–70.

36. Ibid., *Clackamas*.

37. Ibid., *Maurice Shaw*.

38. Ibid., *Winnie, Ocean Maid*. Were these Maryland Agnews any relation to Spiro T. Agnew, President Richard Nixon's vice president, also from Maryland? Spiro Agnew was forced out of office for corruption and replaced by Gerald T. Ford.

39. Ibid., *Hiawatha, Whippoorwill, Ida C. Robinson*. A Brooklyn grocery in the 1920s was owned and operated by Black Hand extortionist Lupo "the Wolf" Saietta and his son, after his release from prison. Was this the *Bonafide* one?

40. Ibid., *Mary H. Diebold*.

41. Ibid., *Cherrie, Shooter's Island*. See also *I'm Alone*.

Chapter 3. Landfall Manhattan

1. Ambrose Lightship, replaced by an electronic rig on stilts, can be visited at the South Street Seaport Museum at Piers 15–17 in the East River.

2. NARA, R.G. 26, *Josephine K.*, *Brooklyn*, and *Dauntless*. See also Willoughby, *Rum Wars*, 144–145.

3. NARA, R.G. 26, *Zelda*, *Strandhill*. *Cherrie* had the same French captain as the *Zelda*.

4. Ibid., *Ohio*, *Alexander*.

5. See the single index entry for New York City in Willoughby, *Rum Wars*.

6. Ibid., *Winnie*, *Robert C. Lowry*.

7. Ibid., *Rescue*, *Klip*. See Asbury, *The Great Illusion*, 245, for harbor chases and Wolf, *Costello*, 72.

8. Ibid., *Orduna* (British) and *Deutschland*, *Oriziba*, *Thuringia*, and *Albert Ballin* (German ships). See also Livingtone, *Belle Out of Order*.

9. Ibid., *Surf*; and Willoughby, *Rum Wars*, 152, and *New York News*, 6.21.1927.

10. Ibid., *Pegasus*, *Nomad*, *Wanderer*, *Cocoon*, *Grey Goose*.

11. Ibid., *Restless*.

12. Ibid., *Modesty/Flamingo* owned by Christopher Byrnes of Long Island.

13. Op. cit. *Modesty*, clipping for 10.22.1927.

14. NARA, R.G. 26, *Arlyn* and Willoughby, *Rum Wars*, 114.

15. Ibid., *Rosemary*.

16. Ibid., *Ekers*. The Kinder gang both owned and operated: *Butetown*, *Shooter's Island*, *I'm Alone*, *Elma*, *Hohenlinden/Penlinden*, *Cherrie*. The sinking of the *I'm Alone* in the Gulf of Mexico by the Coast Guard and the shooting death of one of its crewmen led to an international case involving Great Britain, France, and Canada, which all had an interest in the incident as owners of the boat, or of its cargo, or as the country of the deceased.

17. Ibid., *Loretta*, *Holmewood* pretending to be *Texas Ranger* and Willoughby, *Rum Wars*, 71–72 and 115–116. The *Litchfield* was seized off Yonkers.

18. Ibid., *Rescue*.

19. Ibid., *Warbug*.

20. Ibid., *Raritan Sun*.

21. See NARA, R.G. 26, *Annie Louise*, *Ruth Mildred*, and *Mary of New Bedford*, and Misc. C. boat file. Also see McGill interview, 9.23.1928, by St. Clair McElway in the *New York Herald Tribune*. Smuggling to the fish market was so brazen that longshoremen, unloading the liquor at night, asked police on patrol to help unload saying they were all on the same payroll, according to Katz, *Uncle Frank*, 72.

22. Ibid., *Nerissa*.

23. Ibid., *Quaco Queen*.

24. Ibid., *Lynx II*, *Warbug*, Willoughby, *Rum Wars*, 45. Rum boats dock-ing here probably included: *Augusta*; *Thomas: Arthur*; *Giant King*; *Ellice B.*; *Doran*; *Catherine Moulton*; *Helen*; *May B.*; *Klip*; *Kingfisher*; *Toxaway*; *Ravin II*; *M.S. Quay III*; *Atalanta*; *Isit*; *Dorothy*; *Vee*; *Warbug*; *Man-o-War*; *Rosemary*; *Lynx II*; and *Aphrodite*.

25. Ibid., *Ohio*, *Robert Lowry*, *Corone*, *Donetta*. White and Willensky, *AIA Guide to NYC*, 6 and 8, says the Customs Barge Office was built on the east edge of Battery Park in 1880 and rebuilt there in 1914. Today the U.S. Coast Guard occupies the site in a "buff, bland" building with a bayfront, which is "an unfortunate" structure in a prominent location according to *AIA Guide to NYC*.

26. Ibid., *Underwriter*, *Dorothy*, and Willoughby, *Rum Wars*, 148, and Katz, *Uncle Frank*, 73.

27. Ibid, *Trader*. See also *Clara Mathieu* and the federal case in Manhattan against Browne-Willis c. 1927. Also Willoughby, *Rum Wars*, 36 and 55–59.

28. NARA, R.G. 56, Entry 191, *Albertina* for interview of Prohibition Agent Thomas Guilfoyle with Jeffries 11.24.1926 and see R.G. 26, *Marion Phyllis*, for nonmonetary transactions on Rum Row. When Ralph Capone, 87 Varick Street, Manhattan, called to learn the fate of the *Albertina*, his name and address were recorded although authorities as yet had no idea he was Al Capone's older brother.

29. NARA, R.G. 26, *Winona* (Captain Stone).

30. Ibid., *Amoy* and *Fantasma* (Captain Rhoades).

31. Ibid., *Reliance*, (Captain Newton), *Augusta* and *Zelda* (Captain Snow), *William Maloney* (Captain Jenkins), *Josephine* (Captain Cluett), *Raritan Sun* (Captain Ford), *Kingfisher* (Captain Tanos), and *Wydabiity* (Captain Crawford).

32. Ibid., *Dorothy M. Smart*, *Quaco Queen*. The Seaman's Church Institute began in 1834 as a chapel on a barge at the Coenties Slip on the East River. After Prohibition it was at 17 State Street where nineteenth-century *Moby Dick* author Herman Melville was born. Today it is at 74 Trinity Place #1414. The Titanic Memorial, on the roof of the Seaman's Institute during Prohibition, sur-vives as a monument in Titanic Memorial Park on Fulton Street between Pearl and Water Streets according to *AIA Guide to NYC*, 10, 23, 31.

33. Ibid., *William A. Morse*, *Lynx II*, *Mascot*.

34. Ibid., *Lorraine Rita*, originally the *Albatross*. Its crew included: Kline Hornung; N. Olsen; Alec Freedberg; Walter Hagen; Ennis Lemp; Captain Charles Sawyer; Otto Holeman; Frank Welch; John Smith; Henry Fisher; and Frank Guilbert.

35. Ibid., *Missoe* (Romero) and *Winona* (Levy and Regno).

36. Ibid., *Arlyn* (sugar freighter), *Julito* and *Atalanta* (Supercargo Bitters), *Metak* (Supercargo Ferguson), *Dorin* (Supercargo Smith), *William A. Morse* (Supercargo Pond) and NARA, R.G. 56, *Albertina*.

37. NARA, R.G. 26, *Sebastopol/Westmoreland.*

38. Ibid., *Sebastopol/Westmoreland.* A lower court dismissed the case, a circuit court reversed it, and the Supreme Court upheld the reversal.

Chapter 4. The Broadway Mob

1. Stephen Graham, *New York Nights* (New York: Doran, 1927). Old British beer houses served ale and wine in a separate room close to the porch or "bower," which may be the origin of the word Bowery, or it is from the Dutch word *bur* meaning *buttery,* which was made on the porch? Erdoes, *1000 Remarkable Facts about Booze* (New York: Rutledge, 1981), 31. See White and Willensky, *AIA Guide to NYC* (New York: Oxford Press, 2010), 203, for McGurk's Suicide Hall.

2. See Izzy Einstein, *Prohibition Agent #1* (New York: Stokes, 1932); Herbert Asbury, *The Great Illusion,* 239; and Jenna Weissman Joselit, *Our Gang: Jewish Crime and the New York Jewish Community 1900–1940* (Bloomington, IN: Indiana University Press, 1983); and *AIA Guide to NYC,* 697.

3. For Rothstein, see Donald H. Clarke, *In the Reign of Rothstein* (New York: Vanguard, 1929); Leo Katcher, *The Big Bankroll: Life and Times of Arnold Rothstein* (New York: De Capo, 1994); and Carolyn Rothstein, *Now I'll Tell* (New York: Vanguard, 1934).

4. Martin Meyer, *Emory Buckner* (New York: Harper & Row, 1968), 195–196. Walker, *Night Club Era,* 62, mentions the murder of four government witnesses at the time of Gordon's trial for income tax evasion in 1933. See Carl Sifakis, *Mafia Encyclopedia* for entries on Waxey Gordon, Joe Reinfeld, and Abner "Longy" Zwillman, reportedly a partner with Seagram's Distilleries in Canada in the 1930s. Reinfeld worked with Gordon during Prohibition, and Zwillman and he bought Somerset Ltd. (founded 1934) from Joseph Kennedy c. 1944. In the 1950s, Zwillman died in the basement of his West Orange, New Jersey home, ostensibly a suicide.

5. See Irving Howe and Kenneth Libo, *How We Lived: A Documentary History of Immigrant Jew in America 1890–1930* (New York: Richard Marek, 1979) for information that Orgen's orthodox Jewish family disowned him after he became a gangster. Sifakis, *Mafia Encyclopedia,* reports that Lepke was the richest man to die in the electric chair.

6. See Hank Messick, *Lansky* (New York: Putnam, 1971); Albert Fried, *Rise and Fall of the Jewish Gangster in America* (New York: Holt, Rinehard, Winston, 1980); and Joselit, *Our Gang,* 88, cites Mark Haller's "Bootleggers in American Gambling 1920–50," *Commission on Review of National Policy toward Gambling in America* (1976) as the source for the fact 50 percent of gangsters during Prohibition were Jewish.

7. See Sifakis, *Mafia Encyclopedia* for entry on Schultz and see Rufus Schatzberg, *Black Organized Crime in Harlem 1920–30* (New York: Garland, 1993).

8. See T. J. English, *Paddy-Whacked: The Untold Story of the Irish-American Gangster* (New York: HarperCollins, 2005). Also see Sifakis, *Mafia Encyclopedia*, 341–342, for entries under "Waterfront" and "White Hand" for references to Irish gangsters; Lee, *How Dry*, 119.

9. The *Ellice B.*, a Dwyer ship, was suspected of robbing the *Veronica*.

10. For more on Dwyer ships and boats, see NARA, R.G. 26, *Dick, Dorin, Augusta, Timothy, Alexander, Clark A. Corkum, Ellice B.*

11. Ibid., *Augusta*.

12. Ibid., *Metak*.

13. Ibid., *Elma, Mulhouse*.

14. Ibid., *Walter Holkien, Vincent White, Lynx II, Clackemas*. See also Willoughby, *Rum Wars*, 162 and English, *Paddy-Whacked*, 112, for techniques used by Dwyer's syndicate to corrupt others.

15. Sifakis in *Mafia Encyclopedia* maintains that Madden is unique as a WASP gangster, but T. J. English in *Paddy-Whacked* notes that Madden was Irish-American, his parents had emigrated from Ireland to England where he was born. According to English, Madden told his lawyer in a private conversation years after Prohibition that he served Joe Kennedy's liquor in his Prohibition-era clubs.

16. Fay usually wore a bulletproof vest but was not wearing it when he was shot: possibly he never expected a doorman to be a danger? For Fay and Higgins, see Sifakis, *Mafia Encyclopedia*; Stanley Walker, *Night Club Era* (New York: Stokes, 1933); English, *Paddy-Whacked*, and Lee, *How Dry*, 126.

17. See George Wolf with Joseph DiMorra, *Frank Costello: Prime Minister of the Underworld* (New York: William Morrow, 1974) and Leonard Katz, *Uncle Frank*, 77, mentions that police detective Rudolph McLaughlin watched Costello in the 1920s and reported seeing him in the company of Jews and Irish gangsters but had no idea he was also connected with Italians. Luciano believed the Mob was helped by having an Italian with an Irish name given the fact that a majority of police and politicians in the city were Irish.

18. See Giuseppe Selvaggi, translated by William A. Packer, *The Rise of the Mafia in New York through World War II* (Indianapolis, IN: Bobbs Merrill, 1978), 104, for a list of freighters.

19. See Martin Gosch and Richard Hammer, *Last Testament of Lucky Luciano* (Boston: Little, 1974); Humbert S. Nelli, *The Business of Crime: Italians and Syndicate Crime in the United States* (New York: Oxford, 1976); Alyn Brodsky, *The Great Mayor: Fiorello La Guardia* (New York: St. Martin's, 2003), 281 on Marinelli; Thomas A. Repetto, *American Mafia: A History of its Rise to Power* (New York: Holt, 2004); and Selvaggi, *Rise of the Mafia*.

20. See James Lardner and Thomas Repetto, *New York Police Department: A City and Its Police* (New York: Holt, 2000) and *New York Times*, 11.29.1922. See Katz, *Uncle Frank*, 56 for mention of the Curbside Exchange, managed by Tommy "The Bull" Pennochio for Masseria. See also Asbury, *Great Illusion*, 229 and Buckner's *1926 Congressional Testimony* for information that: 95 percent of liquor from sixteen licensed distilleries was diverted to the black market during Prohibition; one hundred illegal cutting plants in brownstone tenements throughout the city went into operation after midnight; and medicinal liquor was diverted from the city's 1,200 drug stores. Supposedly Italian homes in New York City provided eight times more bootlegged liquor than all the distilling plants.

21. Sifakis, *Mafia Encyclopedia*, 286. See Virgil W. Peterson, *The Mob: 200 Years of Organized Crime in New York* (Ottawa, IL: Green Hill, 1983); Craig Thompson and Alan Raymond, *Gang Rule in New York* (New York: Dial, 1940).

22. See Van De Water, *McCoy*, 37–38, and 275, and NARA, R.G. 26, *Strandhill*. Masseria insisted that Lucania prove his loyalty on the spot by robbing the Corn Exchange Bank on 37th Street and Luciano was caught. Costello's influence with the police got the charges dropped. After that, Lucania's primary loyalty was to Costello. See Gosch and Hammer, *Last Testament of Lucky Luciano*.

23. U.S. Senate, 69th U.S. Congress, *Proceedings of the Judiciary Subcommittee on the National Prohibition Law*, April 1926, and Martin Mayer, *Emory Buckner* (New York: Harper & Row, 1968).

24. See Sifakis, *Mafia Encyclopedia*, 126, on Yale's funeral. See also Lee, *How Dry*, 128–129. Adonis eventually ruled the mafia in Brooklyn.

25. See Sifakius, *Mafia Encyclopedia*, 258, for Petrosino.

26. Craig Thompson and Alan Raymond, *Gang Rule in New York* (New York: Dial Press, 1940), 90–91. See Lerner, *Dry Manhattan*, for more on the sting operation. Inexplicably, an illegal speakeasy continued at this same location for another year.

27. See *New York Chronology*, 392, on Lindy's. See NARA, R.G. 10, *National Commission on Prohibition*, Box 207, where Coast Guard Captain Lauriat told the Wickersham Commission that Chase National Bank of New York financed smuggling. See also Carolyn Rothstein, *Now I'll Tell* (New York, Vanguard, 1934), 71, 101, 161. She claimed her husband never had to post collateral for bank loans.

28. See Rothstein, *Now I'll Tell*, 159 and *New York Herald Tribune*, 8.23.1924.

29. See NARA, R.G. 10, National Commission on Prohibition, Box 207 and Sifakis, *Mafia Encyclopedia*, 286. Rothstein, *Now I'll Tell*, mentioned that Arnold Rothstein told social friends, who did not realize the extent of his underworld connections, that the government position he felt most qualified to

fill was NYPD Police Commissioner! (He often knew before the police when crimes had been committed and by whom.) For Foley Square, see *AIA Guide to NYC*, 79. See also Craig Thompson and Allan Raymond, *Gang Rule*, 69, and James Lardner and Thomas Repetto, *New York Police Department: A City and Its Police* (New York: Holt and Co., 2000), 199.

    30. Sifakis, *Mafia Encyclopedia*, 266–267.

Chapter 5. Scofflaw City

    1. See Asbury, *Great Illusion*, 211. Information for night clubs was culled from a variety of sources, the most important were Al Hirshfeld, *Manhattan Oasis* (New York: Dutton, 1932), republished in 2003 as *Speakeasies of 1932* (Milwaukee, WI; Glenn Young Books); Stanley Walker's *Night Club Era* (New York: Stokes, 1933); Izzy Einstein *Prohibition Agent #1* (New York: Frederick Stokes, 1932); Michael Lerner, *Dry Manhattan* (Cambridge: Harvard, 2007); Stephen Longstreet, *City on Two Rivers* (New York: Hawthorne, 1975); Stephen Graham's *New York Nights* (New York: Doran, 1927); Shaw, *52nd Street* (New York: Da Capo, 1971); Kenneth Jackson, ed., *Encyclopedia of New York City* (New Haven, CT: Yale University Press, 1995); Henry Lee, *How Dry We Were* (Englewood, NJ: Prentice Hall, 1963); Robert Sylvester, *No Cover Charge: A Backward Look at the Night Club* (New York: Dial Press, 1956); James Trager, ed., *New York Chronology* (New York: HarperCollins, n.d.).

    Lerner in *Dry Manhattan*, 132, explains that mapping clubs and speakeasies is impossible because most dwelled in the shadows, rarely kept records, and often relocated and changed their names after raids. This chapter's organization relies on Lerner's observation that resistance to Prohibition began in immigrant and working-class neighborhoods, then spread to the middle class by the mid-1920s, and then to Harlem.

    2. For Lamb's Club, see Lerner, *Dry Manhattan*, and Walker, *Night Club Era*. For *Racquet and Tennis Club*, see *Chronology of New York*, 398, and *AIA Guide to NYC*. While Mullan-Gage was in effect, 1921–1923, it was illegal for New Yorkers to transport liquor in flasks.

    3. Martin Meyer, *Emory Buckner* (New York: Harper & Row, 1968), 190; Morris Markey and John Bull, *That's New York* (New York: Macy-Masius, 1927); NARA, R.G. 26, *Elma*.

    4. See Lerner, *Dry Manhattan*, 74; Traeger, *New York Chronology*, entry for 1930; and NARA, R.G. 26, *Entrophy* (*Walucia III*). Buckner padlocked the old Brevoort Hotel in Greenwich Village before backing off hotels.

    5. Joseph Mitchell, *McSorley's Wonderful Saloon* (New York: Pantheon, 1992). If the Bowery had "John the Baptist," Greenwich Village had the

drunken "Archbishop of Canterbury" who once mistook the lights in front of Mayor Walker's home for the entrance to the subway and, when he couldn't get in, smashed them to bits.

6. Peter Kriendler with Paul Jeffers, '21: Everyday was New Year's Eve (Dallas, TX: Taylor, 1999).

7. Bruce Kayton, Radical Walking Tour of New York (New York: Seven Stories, 2003) and AIA Guide to NYC, 184.

8. Mary Kingsbury Simkhovitch, My Story of Greenwich Village (New York: Norton, 1928); Caroline Ware, Greenwich Village 1920–30 (New York: Harper & Row, 1965); Edmund Wilson, American Earthquake (New York: Doubleday, 1958).

9. Lee, How Dry, 56.

10. Longstreet, City Between Two Rivers, 216, said 45th was the "wettest" in the United States.

11. See Artie Shaw, 52nd Street; Kriendler with Jeffers, 21, and Babette Rosamond, Robert Benchley (New York: Paragon House, 1970). David Niven, a young, unemployed actor looking for work in New York City in 1934, was hired to sell the new 21 Club brand of liquor after repeal.

12. Belle Livingstone, Belle Out of Order (New York: Holt, 1959).

13. Gilbert Maxwell, Helen Morgan (New York: Hawthorne, 1967), 52 and 86.

14. Lee, How Dry, 61.

15. For Harlem, see James Weldon Johnson, Black Manhattan (New York: Da Capo, 1991); Claude McKay, Home to Harlem (Boston: Northeastern University Press, 1987); Alan Shoener, ed., Harlem on My Mind: 1900–1968 (New York: Random House, 1968); Edmund Wilson, American Earthquake (New York: Doubleday, 1958); Lerner, Dry Manhattan, and Graham, New York Nights. Note: Lenox Avenue is now Malcolm X Boulevard, Seventh Avenue, north of Central Park, is Adam Clayton Powell Jr. and Eighth Avenue is Frederick Douglass Boulevard.

16. Lerner, Dry Manhattan, 223.

17. Langston Hughes, Langston Hughes Reader (New York: George Brazilla, 1958); Carl Van Vechten, Nigger Heaven (Urbana, IL: University Press, 2000, original edition 1926). According to AIA Guide to NYC, 541, the top six floors of the nine-story Thurgood Marshall Academy, on the southwest corner of 135th and Adam Clayton Powell Jr. Boulevard, were built over the original Small's Paradise.

18. Ethel Waters with Charles Samuels, His Eye Is on the Sparrow (New York: Doubleday, 1951).

19. See Billy Rose, Wine, Women and Words (New York: Simon & Schuster, 1946).

20. For Broderick, see Arnold Shaw, 52nd Street (New York: Da Capo, 1971), 52 and 56; Fowler, Beau James; Walsh, Gentleman Jimmy Walker; Damon

Runyon, *Omnibus* (Garden City, NY: Sun Dial Press, 1944); and James Lardner and Thomas Repetto, *NYPD*.

21. See Ralph Blumenthal, *The Stork Club: America's Most Famous Night-spot and the Lost World of Cafe Society* (Boston: Little, Brown, 2000), 101–102, 113, 118.

22. Herbert Asbury, *Great Illusion*, 277–280; Marion Meade, *Dorothy Parker: What Fresh Hell Is This?* (New York: Villard, 1988); and Graham, *New York Nights*, 69; Erdoes, *1000 Remarkable Facts about Booze*, 34.

23. Edmund Wilson, *American Earthquake* (Garden City, NY: Doubleday, 1958), reprint of 1927 article, 89–91.

Chapter 6. Repeal

1. See Thomas Kessner, *Fiorello LaGuardia and the Making of Modern New York* (New York: McGraw Hill, 1989); Howard Zinn, *LaGuardia in Congress* (New York: Norton, 1969); and Alyn Brodsky, *Great Mayor* (New York: St. Martin's, 2003). La Guardia's father was Italian Catholic and his mother Jewish: they raised their children Episcopalian. La Guardia spoke many languages besides English, including Italian and Yiddish.

2. See Gene Fowler, *Beau James* (New York: Viking, 1969) and George Walsh, *Gentleman Jimmy Walker* (New York: Praeger, 1974), 92–95. The Walker-Gillette Bill of 1920 was nullified by the Supreme Court two weeks after it became law.

3. See James Lardner and Thomas Repetto, *New York Police Department* (New York: Holt, 2000), Lerner, *Dry Manhattan*, 73 and 79, and Morris Markey and John Bull, *That's New York* (New York: Macy-Massius, 1927), 172.

4. A woman's auxiliary to the all-male Association Against the Prohibition Amendment, called the *Molly Pitcher Auxiliary*, demonstrated in New York City in 1923 against the Mullan Gage Act and for its repeal. This is significant as by 1926 New York women had their own organization working for modification and still later for repeal of the 18th. Four other states did not require local and state police to enforce Prohibition either: Montana; Maryland; Nevada; and Wisconsin. Assistant U.S. Attorney General Mabel Walker Willebrandt in *Inside Prohibition* considered such state laws the equivalent of the "Nullification" of federal tariffs in South Carolina by John C. Calhoun in 1830.

5. Hershfeld, *Speakeasies*, 90–91.

6. Op. Cit., *Proceedings of the Senate Subcommittee*, 1926, already cited in chapter 4.

7. See Brodsky, *Great Mayor*, 183, and Lee, *How Dry*, 154.

8. See Lerner, *Dry Manhattan*, for Buckner's urging New York voters before the referendum to "Vote as You Drink." Tuttle's comment appears in Maxwell, *Helen Morgan*.

9. See Walker, *Night Club Era*, and Maxwell, *Helen Morgan*.

10. Kriendler, Peter, *Club 21*, 21 and 33. According to Kriendler, techni-cally this club was not a night club at all but a high-class speakeasy because it had neither floor show nor orchestra.

11. Asbury, *Great Illusion*, 326. Also Lardner and Repetto, *NYPD*, mention the Catholic Archdiocese for Manhattan and the Bronx sent more money to the Vatican than all the dioceses in Europe combined.

12. Sifakis, *Mafia Encyclopedia*, 287, and Virgil W. Peterson, *The Mob* (Ottawa, IL: Green Hill Publishing, 1983), 154.

13. *AIA Guide to NYC*, 295; Lee, *How Dry*, 148.

14. Herbert Hoover, *Memoirs; Cabinet and Presidency 1920–33* (New York: Macmillan, 1952), 278, and U.S. Senate, *Official Records of the National Com-mission on Law Observance and Enforcement*, 71st Congress, 3d Session, Senate Document #307, 1931, also published as the multivolume *Wickersham Report*. See also Asbury, *Great Illusion*, 325. The Jones Act increased penalties for vio-lations of the Volstead Act to $10,000 or five years in prison, with the courts told to discriminate between "casual" and "habitual" violations.

15. See U.S. House of Representatives, *House Record*, May 1, 1929, 756, and January 7, 1930, 1191.

16. Lee, *How Dry*, estimates 100,000.

17. According to Sifakis's entry "Mussolini Shuttle" in the *Mafia Encyclo-pedia*, the shuttle included: Bonano, Maggadinos, Profaci, Coppola, Magliocca, and Maranzano. The killers of Masseria, all in Luciano's gang, were: Siegel; Adonis; Anastasia; and Genovese. (Genovese used trucks from a Queens bakery to delivery liquor during Prohibition.)

18. Op. Cit., *House Record*, 1929 and 1930. Lee, *How Dry*, 197–199. Also see Lerner, *Dry Manhattan*, on Butler's role.

19. See Walker, *Night Club Era*, and Livingstone, *Belle Out of Order*.

20. For statistics, see Willoughby, *Rum Wars*, 158.

21. Lee, *How Dry*, 181. Excellent analysis of WONPR in Lerner, *Dry Manhattan*.

22. See *1000 Facts About Booze*, and Joseph Mitchell, *McSorley's Saloon*, Heywood Broun opined at the time that the increase in coeducation in U.S. colleges and universities caused the disappearance of the old-time saloon more than Prohibition according to Lee, *How Dry*, 181.

23. Lee, *How Dry*, 228.

24. See Joseph Lasch, *Eleanor and Franklin* (New York: Norton, 1971); Ted Morgan, *FDR: A Biography* (New York: Simon & Schuster, 1985); and Herbert Mitgang, *Once Upon a Time in New York: Jimmy Walker and Franklin Roosevelt and the Last Great Battle of the Jazz Age* (New York: Free Press, 2000).

25. See Goosch and Hammer, *Last Testament of Lucky Luciano*. Luciano and Nelli, *The Business of Crime*, 195, mention attendance at the Democratic

convention of 1932. See also Herbert Mitgang, *Once Upon a Time in New York; Jimmie Walker and Franklin Roosevelt and the Last Great Battle of the Jazz Age* (New York: Free Press, 2000), 3. Longstreet, *City on Two Rivers*, 229, claimed FDR delayed asking for Walker's resignation until after the Convention as FDR needed the votes of Tammany delegates supportive of Walker.

26. Jacob Ruppert's suit for damages due to the Volstead Act was rejected by the Supreme Court.

27. See Lee, *How Dry*, 237, for celebrations after the return of real beer, in April, and after repeal in December of 1933.

28. Billy Rose, *Wine, Women and Words* (New York: Simon & Schuster, 1946), 96.

Chapter 7. Manahactanienk

1. Lerner, *Dry Manhattan*, 18, 59–60, 150; Lee, *How Dry*, 178, and Asbury, *Great Illusion*, 61 and 246.

2. Night club and speakeasies mentioned in this chapter were culled from same sources as those mentioned in chapter 5, footnote #1. See Lee, *How Dry*, 122–123, and see also blog posted by Bill Bence on history of Artist and Writers Club at blogspost.com/2010/04.artist-and-writers-restaurant.html.

3. Sifakis, *Mafia Encyclopedia*, 297, and Lee, *How Dry*, 130. Rothstein, according to reporter Donald H. Clarke, enjoyed sparring with the press on accuracy and facts.

4. For Tony's see especially Rosamond, *Robert Benchley*, Meade, *Dorothy Parker*, Kunkel, *Harold Ross*, and Thurber, *Days with Ross*, 127.

5. For primary sources on Guinan, see Walker, *Night Club Era*, and Graham, *New York Nights*, 89–104, and Edmund Wilson, *American Earthquake* (Garden City, NY: Doubleday, 1958), 32–33 Lee, *How Dry*, 192, and Livingtone, *Belle Out of Order*. See also John S. Steen's and Grace Hayward's "Hello Suckers," unpublished manuscript (1941), Billy Rose Collection, New York Public Library.

6. *Wickersham Commission Report*, v. 4, #22; Willoughby, *Rum Wars*, 163. Lerner, *Dry Manhattan*, 150, credits media with a crucial role as does Lee, *How Dry*.

7. See Wolf and DiMorra, *Frank Costello*. Also see Sifakis, *Mafia Encyclopedia* for post-Prohibition histories of gangsters. Joe Stacher, a 1920s associate of Lansky, moved to Israel where the local press referred to him as "*Kosher Nostra*." English in *Paddy-Whacked* and Gore Vidal in *Palimpsest: A Memoir* (New York: Random House, 1995) mention a Joe Kennedy–Costello friendship in the 1940s and 1950s. Ted Schwarz, *Joseph P. Kennedy: The Mogul, the Mob, the Statesman, and the Making of an American Myth* (New York:

Wiley, 2003) and Seymour Hersh, *The Dark Side of Camelot* (Boston: Little, Brown, 1997) also mention a link between the two. Joe Kennedy's father was a pre-Prohibition liquor dealer in Boston and the son started Somerset Ltd. in 1934 after Prohibition ended: dealing in liquor was in the family history. Whether he imported it during Prohibition through Costello and distributed it through Madden remains unproved based solely on the statements of two gangsters.

8. See Fowler, *Beau James*, and Walsh, *Gentleman Jimmy Walker*, and Lerner, *Dry Manhattan*, 99.

9. Richard Erdoes, *1000 Remarkable Facts About Booze* (New York: Rutledge Press, 1981).

10. Unlike most other alcoholic drinks, rum's origins are American and its name derives from *saccharum*, the Latin word for sugar. Erdoes, *Facts About Booze*, 128–129.

11. Ben Yagoda, *About Town: The New Yorker and the World It Made* (New York: Da Capo, 2000), 27. The *Nation* in 1930 reported that half of U.S. urbanites wanted to be New Yorkers. A few authors used as primary sources in this book (Markey, Asbury, McKelway, Longstreet, Wilson, and Hirshfeld) also wrote or were artists for the *New Yorker*.

12. See Erdoes, *Facts About Booze*, p. 41, spells it with an extra h and says it was the source for the name Manhattan as the "place where we all got drunk."

BIBLIOGRAPHY

Primary Sources

Allen, Frederick L. *Only Yesterday.* New York: Harper & Row, 1931.

Asbury, Herbert. *The Great Illusion: An Informal History of Prohibition.* Westport, CT: Greenwood Press, 1968 reprint of 1950 edition.

Chambers, Walter. *Samuel Seabury: A Challenge.* New York: Century Co., 1932.

Clarke, Donald H. *In the Reign of Rothstein.* New York: Vanguard Press, 1929.

Einstein, Izzy. *Prohibition Agent No. 1.* New York: Frederick Stokes Co., 1932.

Graham, Stephen. *New York Nights.* New York: Doran Company, 1927.

Hirschfeld, Al. *Manhattan Oasis.* New York: E.P. Dutton, 1932.

Hoover, Herbert. *Memoirs: Cabinet and Presidency. 1920–33.* New York: Macmillan, 1952.

Hughes, Langston. *Langston Hughes Reader.* New York: George Brazilla Inc., 1958.

Johnson, James W. *Black Manhattan.* New York: De Capo Press, 1991 reprint of 1930 ed.

Kriendler, W. Peter with Paul Jeffers. *"21" Every Day Was New Year's Eve: Memoirs of a Saloonkeeper.* Dallas, TX: Taylor Publishing, 1999.

Kunkel, Thomas, ed. *Letters from the Editor: The New Yorker's Harold Ross.* New York: Random House, 2000.

Lee, Henry. *How Dry We Were.* Englewood Cliffs, NJ: Prentice-Hall, 1963.

Livingstone, Belle. *Belle Out of Order.* New York: Holt, 1959.

Longstreet, Stephen. *City on Two Rivers.* New York: Hawthorne, 1975.

Lythgoe, Gertrude. *The Bahama Queen: Autobiography of Gertrude "Cleo" Lythgoe.* New York: Exposition Press, 1964.

Markey, Morris and John Bull. *That's New York.* New York: Macy-Masius, 1927.

McKay, Claude. *Home to Harlem.* Boston: Northeastern University Press, 1987, reprint of 1928 edition.

Mitchell, Joseph. *McSorley's Wonderful Saloon*. New York: Pantheon, 1992, reprint of 1943 edition.

Rose, Billy. *Wine, Women and Words*. New York: Simon & Schuster, 1946.

Rothstein, Carolyn. *Now I'll Tell*. New York: Vanguard, 1934.

Runyon, Damon. *The Damon Runyon Omnibus*. Garden City, NY: Sun Dial Press, 1944.

Schoener, Allen, ed. *Harlem on My Mind 1900–1968*. New York: Random House, 1968.

Shaw, Artie. *52nd Street: The Street that Never Slept*. New York: Da Capo, 1971.

Simkhovitch, Mary Kingsbury. *Neighborhood: My Story of Greenwich House*. New York: Norton, 1938.

Thurber, James. *The Years with Ross*. Boston: Little, Brown, 1957.

Trager, James, ed. *The New York Chronology*. New York: HarperCollins [n.d.].

U.S. Congress. *Congressional Record*. 1920–1938.

U.S. District Court, Southern New York and Circuit Court of Appeals, second circuit. Prohibition Conspiracy cases against Dwyer et al. and against Browne-Willis. 1926–1927.

U.S. National Archives and Records Administration: Record Group 26, Coast Guard Seized Vessels, entry 179 A-1 and 178, Intelligence Division; Record Group 10, National Commission on Prohibition, Boxes 182, 199, 206–207; Record Group 56, Dept. of Treasury, General Records, entry 191; Record Group 58, Internal Revenue Service Records, entry 231.

U.S. Senate. *Proceedings of Subcommittee [on National Prohibition Law] of Committee on the Judiciary*. April, 1926.

U.S. Senate. *Official Records of the National Commission [Wickersham Commission] on Law Observance and Enforcement*. 71st Congress, 3d Session. Senate Document #307 [1931].

Van de Water, Frederick F. *The Real McCoy* [as told by McCoy]. New York: Doubleday, 1931.

Van Vechten, Carl. *Nigger Heaven*. Urbana, IL: University Press, 2000, original edition 1926.

Vinciguerra, Thomas. *Backward Ran Sentences: The Best of Wolcott Gibbs from the New Yorker*. New York: Bloomsbury Press, 2011.

Walker, Stanley. *The Night Club Era*. New York: Frederick Stokes Co., 1933.

Ware, Caroline. *Greenwich Village 1920–30*. New York: Harper & Row, 1965, reprint of 1935 edition.

Waters, Ethel with Charles Samuels. *His Eye Is on the Sparrow*. New York: Doubleday, 1951.

Willebrandt, Mabel Walker. *Inside Prohibition*. Indianapolis, IN: Bobbs-Merrill, 1929.

Wilson, Edmund. *American Earthquake*. Garden City, NY: Doubleday, 1958, republication of 1927 edition.

Secondary Sources

Allen, Everett S. *The Black Ships: Rum Runners of Prohibition.* Boston: Little, Brown, 1965.

Allsop, Kenneth. *The Bootleggers and Their Era.* New York: Doubleday, 1961.

Behr, Edward. *Prohibition: Thirteen Years that Changed America.* New York: Arcade Publishing, 1996.

Bianco, Anthony. *Ghosts of 42nd Street.* New York: HarperCollins, 2004.

Blumenthal, Ralph. *The Stork Club: America's Most Famous Nightspot and the Lost World of Café Society.* Boston: Little, Brown, 2000.

Brodsky, Alyn. *The Great Mayor: Fiorello LaGuardia and the Making of the City of New York.* New York: St. Martin's Press, 2003.

Burns, Ric and James Sanders, narr. *New York: An Illustrated History.* New York: Knopf, 1999.

Carse, Robert T. *Rum Row.* New York: Rinehart, 1959.

Chambers, Walter. *Samuel Seabury.* New York: Century Co.,1932.

Douglas, Ann. *Terrible Honesty: Mongrel Manhattan in the 1920s.* New York: Farrar, Straus, and Giroux, 1995.

English, T. J. *Paddy Whacked: The Untold Story of the Irish American Gangster.* New York: HarperCollins, 2005.

Erdoes, Richard. *1000 Remarkable Facts About Booze.* New York: Rutledge Press, 1981.

Flotteron, Nicole A. "Rum Running, Bootlegging, Pirates and Prohibition on the East End of Long Island." www.hamptons.com/Home-and-Garden.

Fowler, Gene. *Beau James: The Life and Times of Jimmy Walker.* New York: Viking, 1949.

Fowler, Gene. *Great Mouthpiece: William J. Fallon.* New York: Grosset and Dunlap, 1931.

Fried, Albert. *The Rise and Fall of the Jewish Gangsters in America.* New York: Holt, Rinehart, Winston, 1980.

Gosch, Martin and Richard Hammer. *Last Testament of Lucky Luciano.* Boston: Little Bros., 1975.

Grant, B. J. *When Rum Was King: The Story of the Prohibition Era in New Brunswick.* Fredericton, New Brunswick: Fiddlehead Poetry Books, 1982.

Gunther, Gerald. *Learned Hand: The Man and the Judge.* New York: Knopf, 1994.

Hersh, Seymour. *The Dark Side of Camelot.* Boston: Little, Brown, 1997.

Howe, Irving and Kenneth Libo. *How We Lived: A Documentary History of Immigrant Jews in America 1890–1930.* New York: Richard Marek Pub., 1979.

Jackson, Kenneth T., ed. *Encyclopedia of New York City.* New Haven, CT: Yale University Press, 1995.

Joselet, Jenna Weissman. *Our Gang: Jewish Crime and the New York Jewish Community, 1900–1940*. Bloomington, IN: University Press, 1983.

Josephson, Matthew and Hannah. *Al Smith: Hero of the Cities*. New York: Houghton Mifflin, 1969.

Katcher, Leo. *The Big Bankroll: The Life and Times of Arnold Rothstein*. New York: Da Capo Press, 1994.

Katz, Leonard. *Uncle Frank: The Biography of Frank Costello*. New York: Drake Publishing, 1973.

Kayton, Bruce. *Radical Walking Tours of New York City*. New York: Seven Stories Press, 2003.

Kessner, Thomas. *Fiorello La Guardia and the Making of Modern New York*. New York: McGraw Hill, 1989.

King, John P. *Wicked Tales from the Highlands*, ebook, 2011.

Kunkel, Thomas. *Genius in Disguise: Harold Ross of the New Yorker*. New York: Random House, 1995.

Lardner, James and Thomas Repetto. *New York Police Department: A City and Its Police*. New York: Holt and Co., 2000.

Lasch, Joseph. *Eleanor and Franklin*. New York: Norton and Co., 1971.

Lerner, Michael. *Dry Manhattan*. Cambridge, MA: Harvard University Press, 2007.

Levy, Tedd, "Days of Rum Running in Old Saybrook," *Shoreline Ct. Times*, 11.12.2011.

Linderoth, Matthew. *Prohibition on the Jersey Shore*. Charleston, SC: History Press, 2010.

Maxwell, Gilbert. *Helen Morgan: Her Life and Legend*. New York: Hawthorn, 1967.

Mayer, Martin. *Emory Buckner*. New York: Harper & Row, 1968.

McIllwain, Jeffery Scott. *Organizing Crime in Chinatown: Race, Racketeering in New York City 1890–1910*. Jefferson, NC McFarland, 2004.

Meade, Marion. *Dorothy Parker: What Fresh Hell Is This?* New York: Villard Books, 1988.

Messick, Hank. *Lansky*. New York: Putnam, 1971.

Mitgang, Herbert. *Once Upon a Time in New York: Jimmy Walker and Franklin Roosevelt and the Last Great Battle of the Jazz Age*. New York: Free Press, 2000.

Morgan, Ted. *FDR: A Biography*. New York: Simon & Schuster, 1985.

Nelli, Humbert S. *The Business of Crime: Italians and Syndicate Crime in the United States*. New York: Oxford Press, 1976.

Peterson, Virgil W. *The Mob: 200 Years of Organized Crime in New York*. Ottawa, IL: Green Hill Publishing, 1983.

Repetto, Thomas A. *American Mafia: A History of its Rise to Power*. New York: Holt, 2004.

Rosamond, Babette. *Robert Benchley: His Life and Good Times*. New York: Paragon House, 1970.

Schatzberg, Rufus. *Black Organized Crime in Harlem: 1920–30*. New York: Garland Publishing, 1993.

Schwarz, Ted. *Joseph P. Kennedy: The Mogul, the Mob, the Statesman, and the Making of an American Myth*. Hoboken, NJ: John Wiley & Sons, 2003.

Selvaggi, Giuseppe, translator William A. Packer. *The Rise of the Mafia in New York from 1886 through World War II*. Indianapolis, IN: Bobbs Merrill, 1978.

Sifakis, Carl. *The Mafia Encyclopedia*. New York: Checkmark Books, 1999.

Sylvester, Robert. *No Cover Charge: Backward Look at the Night Club*. New York: Dial Press, 1956.

Thompson, Craig and Alan Raymond. *Gang Rule in New York*. New York: Dial Press, 1940.

Vidal, Gore. *Palimpsest: A Memoir*. New York: Random House, 1995.

Walsh, George. *Gentleman Jimmy Walker*. New York: Praeger, 1974.

White, Norval and Elliot Willensky. *AIA Guide to New York City*. New York: Oxford, 2010.

Willoughby, Malcolm. *Rum War at Sea*. Washington, DC: Government Printing Office. 1964.

Wolf, George with Joseph DiMorra (Dimona). *Frank Costello: Prime Minister of the Underworld*. New York: William Morrow, 1974.

Yagoda, Ben. *About Town: The New Yorker and the World It Made*. New York: Da Capo, 2000.

Zinn, Howard. *La Guardia in Congress*. New York: Norton, 1969.

INDEX

Printed in Great Britain
by Amazon.co.uk, Ltd.,
Marston Gate.